BUILDING A

MILLION DOLLAR

BOOK OF BUSINESS

PRINCIPLES AND BEHAVIORS
FOR A
SUCCESSFUL LAW PRACTICE

Daniel P. Lynch, Esq.

BUILDING A MILLION DOLLAR BOOK OF BUSINESS
PRINCIPLES AND BEHAVIORS FOR A SUCCESSFUL LAW PRACTICE

To contact Dan:

Website ....:	www.LynchLaw-Group.com
Email ....:	DLynch@LynchLaw-Group.com
LinkedIn ....:	www.linkedin.com/in/danielplynch1/
Phone ....:	724-776-8000

To contact the publisher, inCredible Messages Press, visit www.inCredibleMessages.com

Printed in the United States of America

ISBN 978-0-9976056-8-6 paperback
ISBN 978-0-9976056-9-3 eBook

Book Coach ....:	Bonnie Budzowski
Cover Design ......:	Bobbie Fratangelo

DEDICATION

THIS BOOK IS DEDICATED to my kids, Danny, Katie, Jessica, and Stephanie, in the hope that they will find guidance, value, and wisdom in my words.

ACKNOWLEDGMENTS

I WOULD LIKE TO ACKNOWLEDGE a number of people who helped make this book a reality.

First, I want to recognize my parents, Joe and Nadia Lynch, for raising me in an environment that gave me the foundation for the ideas found in this book. They instilled in me a work ethic that has helped me get to where I am today and what I later refer to in this book as grit quotient. They always supported my entrepreneurial inclinations and gave me the freedom and courage to follow those dreams.

Second, I would like to thank my wife, Susan, for her never-ending support. For the last twenty-six years, she has helped me to frame my life in the manner to which it has become, positioning me to be able to write the content of this book. For the last three years, Susan has enabled me to be able to experience life in a way that has given me the ability to write this book. Susan also contributed her intellect and editing skills to the final version of this book.

Third, I thank my book coach, Bonnie Budzowski. Without her skill in book writing, guidance, and persistent "drive," this book would never have been finished.

Next, I would like to recognize my brother Joe for his wisdom, interest, thought-provoking questions, and editing that provided the fine-tuning of the content of this book, but more importantly for the confidence his comments gave me in publishing this book.

Finally, I would like to thank my colleague, Mike Oliverio, for his editing skills and legal prowess, which made the final drafts of my transcript a better product for publication.

As much as this book is intended to teach lawyers how to build a book of business, in many ways this book is for my children: Danny, Katie, Jessica, and Stephanie. Much as a spouse frames your life and helps you to evolve into the person you become (twenty-seven years ago my grandmother predicted my wife, Susan, would be the making of me), children do the same. At every stage, our children have had questions that have challenged Susan and me. They have had experiences, some good and some bad, that have impacted how I've grown older. My children have made me want to provide for them and to be the best person I can be. I want to be proud of my kids. I want them to be great, and I want them to be successful. But most importantly, I want them to be the best they can be, and I want them to be happy.

Long before I had kids, or even a marriage, I read Shakespeare's *Hamlet*. I was struck by the passage in which Hamlet's best friend, Polonius, gives advice to his son, Laertes, on how to live life. This is one of my favorite passages of any book I have ever read, and the one I quote the most. It is a touching scene and one that every parent can relate to.

The book in your hands is an outline of how I have lived my life. It is a story about perseverance and success, providing a methodology for how to achieve. Although this book is written for lawyers, I believe it transcends all professional services and can even serve as an inspiration for life in general. If something drastic were to happen to me and I were unable to see my kids into adulthood, these are the words I would want my kids to hear. It is my effort at a father's instructional booklet on life.

POLONIUS'S ADVICE TO HIS SON, LAERTES

~ From Shakespeare's *Hamlet*

This is Polonius's advice to his son as Laertes is about to
board a ship to France, where he will attend university.

Yet here, Laertes! Aboard, aboard, for shame!

The wind sits in the shoulder of your sail,

And you are stay'd for. There; my blessing with thee!

And these few precepts in thy memory

See thou character. Give thy thoughts no tongue,

Nor any unproportioned thought his act.

Be thou familiar, but by no means vulgar.

Those friends thou hast, and their adoption tried,

Grapple them to thy soul with hoops of steel;

But do not dull thy palm with entertainment

Of each new-hatch'd, unfledged comrade. Beware

Of entrance to a quarrel, but being in,

Bear't that the opposed may beware of thee.

Give every man thy ear, but few thy voice;

Take each man's censure, but reserve thy judgment.

Costly thy habit as thy purse can buy,

But not express'd in fancy; rich, not gaudy;

For the apparel oft proclaims the man,

And they in France of the best rank and station

Are of a most select and generous chief in that.

Neither a borrower nor a lender be;

For loan oft loses both itself and friend,

And borrowing dulls the edge of husbandry.

This above all: to thine own self be true,

And it must follow, as the night the day,

Thou canst not then be false to any man.

Farewell: my blessing season this in thee!

CONTENTS

CHAPTER 1

THE SHAPING OF A LAW PRACTICE

B Y AT LEAST ONE OBJECTIVE MEASURE, I'm a success at building a book of business. My annual originations since 2008 have been in excess of $1 million, when the typical lawyer stands at $200,000 to $300,000.

As founder and managing partner of The Lynch Law Group, it's in my best interest to share the secrets of my success with my team. As such, we devote an hour and a half every other week at The Lynch Law Group to a practice development meeting. Over the years of my legal career, I have devoted a great deal of thought to uncovering and articulating the principles and behaviors that generate and sustain an above-average book of business.

When I reflect on the broad scope of my 25-plus year career as a lawyer, two events come to mind. The first event occurred when I was only 15 years old, emerging as an adult. The other event is so fresh it still stings. These two events might serve as bookends, pulling back the curtain on my approach to life and lawyering. Each of the events involves both attitude and action.

At age 15 I was a counselor at a Boy Scout camp. A group of us was given two tasks: moving tables and cleaning the latrines. Like typical teenagers, the boys around me moaned and whined. The tables were heavy, and the latrines stunk. The day was hot, and we were sweaty. With rebellious adolescence, the boys complained and articulated their dissatisfaction with the camp director and other authority figures.

I didn't understand or join the whining. The work had to be done, so I thought we should make it fun. To that end, I started horsing around, amping things up, and created a challenge. How fast could we move the tables? Could we hold our breath the entire time we cleaned any given toilet—and still do a good job? These contests influenced everyone's attitudes by creating a positive atmosphere.

The challenge energized the group as we did our work, and we had a lot of fun with each other. We sang. We joked. We laughed. The tough job got done, and we finished with satisfaction, fresh bonds, and a positive attitude.

Fast forward to 2014. I was 47 years old and had been running a successful practice for 13 years. I had what I thought was a solid legal team in place. I believed that working and living intentionally had led to success, and I often articulated principles of success to my team members and my children.

Things were going so well that my wife and I were pondering how to take our four children on a year-long trip. One day in August, when I came to the office after being away for a long weekend, I got the shock of a lifetime.

At 8:55 on that Monday morning, I walked into my office, expecting to gather my things for a nine o'clock meeting with my book coach. Without notice, the five partner-level lawyers of the Firm came into my office, and one of them announced, "We're leaving."

Taken off guard, I replied, "You're leaving? What do you mean?"

He answered, "We are leaving and starting our own firm." It was indeed a Caesar-esque moment.

At one point, I said, "Is there anything we can do to talk about this?"

One answered, "No. We are too far down the road."

As I walked into the conference room to meet my book coach, I certainly didn't feel as if I had any right to write a book. I remember sitting down with my arms hanging, feeling overwhelmingly helpless. It was like the feeling you get in a dentist chair when you've resigned yourself to endure what you can't control.

I felt shocked and betrayed, as if everything I had worked for had disappeared in a moment. The people I had mentored, taught, and brought along to the point they had reached, had left me. Over the weekend, while I was away, this group of five had cleaned out their offices and prepared to leave without notice. They had obviously been planning their exit for months.

I wasn't scared about making a living, but I did feel like a failure. I felt that I should have seen this event coming and averted it—or not allowed it to manifest in the first place.

Over the next several days, the group who left recruited others to join them: an associate, paralegal, receptionist, and controller. Only a secretary, marketing director, paralegal, three associates, and I remained. By headcount, I had lost more than 50 percent of my firm.

My biggest hang-up involved how this event would reflect on my reputation and me. How would the legal community perceive me? Was I a failure?

I felt violated in a deep and profound sense. This feeling was coupled with the sense that I was somehow to blame, that it was somehow my fault. Working through my feelings of failure took six months to a year, and the experience still stings.

In the months following this event, I reflected on the words I often told my kids: The true mettle of a person is revealed when his or her chips are down, not when things are going well. The question was, what attitude and actions would I take now when everything seemed to have gone south, when people whom I trusted had betrayed me, and when my plans were more than disrupted? Would I become distrustful and bitter? Was this the beginning of the end?

Even as I struggled, I knew at a deep level that this event, in addition to being a crisis, was also an opportunity to clarify and test my own attitudes and actions about success. Was I all talk, or did I have genuine insights about success? Would I stop growing because of this setback or live out the lessons I was constantly parroting to my team, my children, and myself?

For me, I didn't have much of a choice. I was numb. I was on autopilot. I had a wife who worked occasionally at the office and four young children. I accepted the challenge, even as I was hurting, at least on the practical level of building the Firm back up. I had, and still have, an amazing network of friends, all of whom are clients and referral sources. These individuals helped me analyze my situation, work through the head trash that attempted to consume me, and keep me on track to be the person I am. One of those friends summarized it poignantly, "This event does not define you. This is not the last chapter of your life's book." To all of those friends, I will be forever grateful.

With this backdrop of encouragement, I got busy. It is amazing what you can accomplish when you take the view that you have no choice. First, I asked myself some basic questions about what I have always believed to be true, even from my Boy Scout days. Some of the questions may surprise you, and some may be questions you have asked yourself. Answers to these fundamental questions would set the direction as I rebuilt my team.

- Is it possible to make lawyering fun and successful?

- Is it possible in this business to build relationships that satisfy?

- What elements make up a winning business strategy and practice?

- How do I build a professional, productive, and loyal team?

- How do I get work done for clients while chasing new business?

- Assuming it is ineffective to sell on price and quality (because everyone does), how do I distinguish myself?

- How do I build a network that feeds me business rather than simply taking up my time?

- Do today's clients want transactions or experiences? How do I deliver the latter?

- What's the right balance between the personal and professional? How do I achieve this balance in the hours I have each week?

In answering these questions, I remembered the actions I took to build my book of business and the practice in the first place. I had researched, tested, and perfected these behaviors over the years, and they worked. At the same time, I knew behaviors are incomplete without principles or attitudes to undergird them. Adherence to bedrock principles provides the fortitude you need to stay on task and keep moving forward in the face of bad days, weeks, even months, repeated rejection, or outright betrayal. Principles also keep you grounded and genuine; the ones who try to fake it are eventually exposed.

As I reflected on my situation and debated the answers to these questions within myself, I recruited and hired. I did what I had always done to build a team and build a business. As this book goes to print, over three years have elapsed since the betrayal. The Firm has nearly twice as many lawyers, more staff, and more revenue than we did at the time of the event. The members of the Firm are a much better fit.

I have accepted ownership of things I might have done differently, and I have clarified and recommitted myself to the things I stand for, including the need to earn a partnership-level vote.

Those who stayed with the Firm (all of whom, I'm thankful to report, stepped up their game) have said, "Thank God that group left. This is a better place to be." My wife says I'm a happier person and a better husband and father. My executive coach says I'm a better leader. Perhaps the best evidence is that The Lynch Law Group has been voted by its employees to be one of the top 100 "Best Places to Work" in a survey conducted by the *Pittsburgh Business Times* in each of the two years following the betrayal.

Now I feel time-and-hardship tested, ready to share what I've learned with you. You'll discover that my central principle is that, above all, lawyering is a relationship business. A good lawyer knows the law and applies the law as an art on behalf of people. As you read this book, you'll discover that I invest a great deal of time, energy, and money in face-to-face interactions with clients and referral sources. I strive to make those interactions sincere, creative, and fun. I treat every client as a friend who deserves a timely response and a personal interest. You won't find tricks and techniques for e-mail or newsletter campaigns. You won't find slick slogans or manipulative techniques to get business. I've built my multimillion-dollar business through face-to-face encounters with people. I'll tell you how I've done it, and I sincerely believe that you can do it too.

WHAT TO EXPECT FROM THIS BOOK

Every action I recommend in this book is intertwined with one or more principles. I thought it fitting, then, to devote the next chapter to an overview of the seven principles you need as a foundation for your efforts to build a book of business and a successful practice.

The rest of this book is divided into sections, each containing short chapters describing a specific action that can lead you to success.

These are the major sections of the book:

- Develop a Clear Focus and Direction

- Set Goals and Hold Yourself Accountable

- Establish a Network

- Perfect Your Pitch

- Every Client Is a Friend and Every Friend Is a Client

- Care and Feeding of Your Clients

- Care and Feeding of Yourself

- Commit to Courage

- Building a Large Practice

CHAPTER 2

PRINCIPLES OF SUCCESS

I F YOU ARE READING THIS BOOK, you are at least curious about what it takes to have a better-than-average book of business, which could lead to a better-than-average law practice. Chances are you are eager to learn techniques, tips, actions, and behaviors that will lead to more clients. You won't be disappointed. I agree that actions and behaviors—consistently practiced over time—are the keys to success. This book will be jammed full of practical, business-building behaviors.

At the same time, I am convinced that the right mindset is a major factor for success in any endeavor. The right mindset enables you to do the following:

- Stick to the behaviors over time

- Embrace rather than dread necessary work

- Enjoy the processes and the people with whom you work

- Strive for excellence rather than taking shortcuts

- Enjoy the journey even as you work like crazy

The right mindset provides the energy and the endurance you need not only to succeed but also to sustain that success.

This chapter, accordingly, is about the mindset and attitudes you need to build a better-than-average book of business, particularly if you want to be reasonably happy in the process. The following seven principles work together synergistically to create a winning mindset.

PRINCIPLE #1: EMBRACE HARD WORK

One of the biggest obstacles to building a million-dollar book of business is the emergence of the I-Want-It-Now generation. I call it the microwave generation. The expectation of instant success is an adolescent mindset, as well as an insult to the ancestors who built our country.

HARD WORK AND PERSEVERANCE
HAVE ALWAYS BEEN THE PATH TO SUCCESS

History is full of examples of those whose achievements were won with hard work. For example, think of the European colonists who settled this continent. Think of the courage and effort needed to leave their home countries and travel to an unknown area in search of a better life.

The offspring of these early settlers were our founding fathers in the American Revolution. These folks worked hard toward their goal of freedom while facing seemingly insurmountable obstacles. One founding father, Benjamin Franklin, asserted, "The way to wealth depends on just two words: industry and frugality."

Lewis and Clark's expedition, The Corps of Discovery, is an excellent example of amazing achievement through hard work. A quarter century after the American Revolution, these men spent two and a half years living off the land, exploring uncharted territory, and experiencing nearly every threat to life a frontiersman could face, while trying to find a waterway from Pittsburgh to the Pacific Ocean. All the while, they were collecting scientific data on the territories' plant and animal life.

Nearly 100 years later, during the turn of the nineteenth century, this country launched and lived through the Industrial Revolution. Men and women traveled great distances from all over the country and world to find work in northern factories, all to make a better life for themselves and their families. In the steel, railroad, automobile, and coal industries, people worked hard to create wealth and the strongest nation in the world. They toiled. They got sick. They were in pain. They saw loved ones prematurely die. What they did not do was complain.

Roughly half a century after the Industrial Revolution, the Greatest Generation defended this country against the Axis powers in WW II. Men died. Women went to work in factories. People worked hard and gave up much to defeat the enemy.

In today's information age, many men and women have engaged in countless hours of hard work to chase dreams and achieve their goals. "Garage-band" companies turned into Fortune 100 companies through sleepless nights, sometimes at the sacrifice of personal relationships and health. Companies like Microsoft, Apple, and Google achieved their success by hard work, not luck.

Our son Danny dreams of playing college baseball. My wife and I must constantly remind him:

> To achieve this goal, you will have to work at it every day for years. Baseball must become a way of life.

Danny wonders why he can't wake up on any given morning and hit the ball 300 feet or run the 60-yard dash in less than 7 seconds. For years, we tried to explain this. Finally, at age 15, and as a freshman in high school, he began to get it. That does not mean Danny practiced the behaviors for as long as it took to achieve his goals, but at least he began to understand the work needed to play the game at a college level. Now at age 18, Danny is currently in the batting cage four or five times a week, in the weight room three or four times a week, and at practice six days a week.

The hardest part is acknowledging that even if Danny does the behaviors, he still might not reach his goal. But does that really matter? Isn't there value in learning hard work? Isn't it more an end in itself, rather than a means to an end? Who wants to go through life wondering, "What if?" What if I would have tried? What if I would have tried out for that team? What if I would have tried out for that part? What if I would have applied for that job?

If hard work is the only way to achieve amazing things, then anyone who decides that he or she wants to build an above-average book of business needs to get his or her head wrapped around the fact that building a successful business is work, and it is hard. As we tell our kids, if something were easy, everyone would do it. This perspective becomes a way of life. It becomes a mind-set or attitude.

Even in high school, I was aware that you can't expect to achieve your goals without hard work and sacrifice. I was a wrestler from 2nd grade to 10th grade. Cutting weight was expected of wrestlers in those days. When I was in 9th grade, I needed to get from 95 pounds to 90. So, while all my buddies were going through puberty, eating double lunches and growing like weeds, I was having a salad or just plain water at the lunch table. This was the dedication required to participate in the sport of my choice.

To build my book of business to exceed $1 million, I've embraced what it took for more than 25 years. I've made developing a practice a way of life. I look to the work to energize me, and I don't complain.

So, what about you? You've already engaged in the discipline needed to get through law school: the outlines, the exams, the grades, law review, moot court, holding down a job, raising a family. Consider all this as the beginning. If you want to set yourself apart from the average, you must continue to work hard.

By the nature of the profession, lawyers are busy people with many responsibilities to clients. An individual lawyer can respond in one of three ways: try to avoid the busyness and responsibilities, tolerate them, or embrace them.

OPTION 1: AVOIDING HARD WORK

Avoiders are not all in. This doesn't mean they are bad people. It simply means they have decided that other areas of their lives require and/or merit more of their attention. Most lawyers that dabble in the practice of law don't have a large book of business, great reputations, or interesting clients.

OPTION 2: TOLERATING HARD WORK

Many lawyers tolerate the work needed to serve clients and develop a practice. They put in the hours to serve clients in a timely fashion. They put up with demanding judges, burdensome deadlines, and obnoxious opposing lawyers. They accept the fact that they must allocate a certain amount of time developing a client base, many times at the expense of their individual interests, their personal relationships, and even their health. Many unfulfilled, unhappy lawyers tolerate the hard work that comes with being a lawyer. But tolerating or accepting is a de-energizing place to be. The hard work feels even harder, the sacrifices seem disheartening and even unfair, and it all leads to an unfulfilled life.

OPTION 3: EMBRACING HARD WORK

All lawyers can choose to embrace the hard work that comes with developing a successful practice. Such lawyers decide that the rigors of a successful practice are fulfilling. They choose to embrace the lifestyle that comes with the profession and even to make it fun. They decide not only to enjoy, but also to find fulfillment and satisfaction in putting in long hours to complete a project.

If you want to build a $1 million book of business, your first step is to decide to embrace the process and the hard work that comes with it. Decide to enjoy the intellectual stimulation associated with tackling a complex issue. Enjoy the argument in front of a judge or with opposing counsel, whether you win or lose. Embrace the challenges associated with demanding clients. Turn practice development into a way of life that is fun for you. Understand that the miserable lawyer on the other side of a case is missing the best part of being a lawyer because that lawyer has chosen to be miserable. You have chosen to "dress up" for your profession. At some point, you will no longer have to make it fun; it will simply be fun. You will enjoy what you do. And you will succeed.

By saying the work will be fun, I'm not trying to sugar-coat it. Some days will take all the determination inside you to keep performing the behaviors that lead to success. On those days, and there will be plenty of them over a career, you'll have to rely on your grit. Angela Duckworth, author of *Grit: The Power of Passion and Perseverance*, defines grit as a combination of passion and perseverance for a singularly important goal. As a math teacher, Duckworth noticed that those who succeeded weren't always the ones with the highest natural ability or IQ. Instead, successful people displayed the most grit. Duckworth went on to become a graduate student and researcher, even creating the "grit scale," which predicted outcomes such as who would graduate from West Point or win the National Spelling Bee.

A 2016 *New York Times* article on Duckworth explains how grit works:

> You cannot will yourself to be interested in something you're not interested in. But you can actively discover and deepen your interest. So once you've fostered an interest, then, and only then, can you do the kind of difficult, effortful, and sometimes frustrating practice that truly makes you better.

You've already demonstrated your interest in law. Now is the time to deepen that interest and embrace the hard work.

PRINCIPLE #2: PURSUE EXCELLENCE

Consider this: You'll find happiness and success in the consistent pursuit of excellence.

The ancient philosophers Socrates, Plato, and Aristotle all wrote and lectured on happiness and the meaning of life. Aristotle was the first to proclaim that happiness is the ultimate purpose of human existence. People have always sought money, pleasure, and "things" to make themselves feel good. Such things may make us feel temporarily happy, but genuine happiness is the ultimate goal, not the sum of things in our lives.

Today, we think of happiness as a state of mind caused by some event, like spending time with friends or family. For Aristotle, though, the pursuit of happiness was the definition of life. Happiness was not a feeling to experience in a few hours. For Aristotle, happiness was the measure of the final value of a person's life in terms of how well that person lived up to his or her full potential. Aristotle said, "It is not one swallow or one fine day that makes a spring, so it is not one day or a short time that makes a man blessed and happy."

A more modern philosopher, Karl Marx, said that man is a creative and productive laborer. Marx hypothesized that industrialized America would fail because workers would not tolerate assembly-line work. The last 100 years have proven him partly right; we see what has happened to the segments of our society that supported industrialized America. We've seen a shift from labor-based production to one supported by technology and robotics. We've seen the transformation from a manufacturing-based economy to a service-based economy.

Taken together, the ideas of Aristotle and Marx lead me to believe that happiness comes in the pursuit of excellence— over a lifetime. Of course, you can't always achieve excellence because, by definition, that measuring stick constantly moves. However, you can work at something to the best of your ability and be great at that thing. Happiness is that sigh of satisfaction, or even a grin, after accomplishing something hard and doing it well, like weeding a garden, finishing a race, or graduating from school. Such moments give us that feeling of creative labor suggested by Marx, and the measure of a valuable life espoused by Aristotle. Looking back after a day, a month, a year, or a lifetime and being able to say, "I did well," is a special kind of happiness.

In our results-oriented culture, it's easy to forget that excellence is a pursuit rather than a single destination. I was reminded of this truth recently concerning our daughter, Katie, age 16. Katie is a passionate and prolific writer. So far, she has written four novels and one poetry collection. When Katie completed her latest novel, I offered to help her connect with professionals who could get the book published or printed.

When Katie didn't respond enthusiastically to my offer, I pushed. Katie resisted. I couldn't understand Katie's reaction because I thought she would get a tremendous sense of accomplishment to see her book in print. Eventually, I learned that many successful novelists have one or more books they never submitted for publication hidden away in a drawer. The authors worked at these books but decided they were not yet up to the standard for publication. That doesn't mean the authors didn't have a sigh or a grin of satisfaction in completing these books. It is just that the book was simply on the road to excellence and not quite there yet.

Katie is enjoying her writing projects at the development level that fits her age and experience. She is learning the pursuit of excellence with each attempt—and enjoying a sense of satisfaction as each book comes to completion.

When someone is engaged in the pursuit of excellence, the journey becomes an end in itself, not the actual goal. An exceptional athlete must enjoy the training, not just playing in the game. A big game hunter who trains and practices for an arduous trip to bag a trophy animal can pleasingly choose not to shoot when he is finally at the top of the mountain with the animal in his sights. In 1984, the British rock band Deep Purple released a song, "Knocking at Your Back Door," with lyrics that capture the essence of this concept: "It's not the kill, it's the thrill of the chase."

There's a lot to be said for doing the right thing (the excellent thing) simply because it is the right thing, not because someone else will see it or judge it. As many of our fathers have said: If it's worth doing, it is worth doing right. It's an issue of character, and your character colors everything you do. Imagine you attempt to toss a tissue or Q-tip into a wastebasket from a distance and miss. Do you leave it there for someone else to pick up? Or do you pick it up yourself?

These ideas may sound philosophical or esoteric—when all you want is to learn how to build a book of business. In my view, excellence and business development are intricately connected. The sense of satisfaction that comes with meaningful tasks and job-well-done experiences energizes you to complete the behaviors needed to build your book of business. Further, a job-well-done mindset results in a standard of excellence that will build your reputation and attract clients.

In our Firm, the mindset of excellence allows us to create a success orientation and a culture of achievement. I consistently talk about the pursuit of excellence in what we do, being vigilant to the highest standards of service. We are a creative and productive law firm, and we define ourselves by the highest degree of service. Our clients and the business community measure us by our results—and also how we provide our services. Carelessness and mediocrity are unacceptable.

Sayings such as, "Whatever," and a defeated, "That's good enough," do not belong in the offices of successful law firms. Rather, we constantly say, "We have to be better today than we were yesterday." The mindset of excellence applies to every area and every task in the Firm. Through the pursuit of excellence, everyone can have a feeling of satisfaction, knowing he or she has done an excellent job—whatever that person's role in contributing to the overall success of the Firm. When each person can say at the end of the day, week, month, year, or career, "We did well," you have the groundwork for success.

PRINCIPLE #3: COMMIT TO KEEPING YOUR WORD

My first boss, Justice James Brickley of the Michigan State Supreme Court, used to say, "If everyone would just say what they are going to do and then do what they say, the world would be a lot better off." This means you need to keep your promises. Don't make a promise you can't keep. And by all means, keep your promises.

Over the years, I have observed lawyers who say they are going to do something and then don't do it, or who don't do it when they say they will. That infuriates clients. Put yourself in their shoes. None of us like it when a contractor tells us he or she will be at our home to install the new air conditioner and then fails to show up. Practicing law is no different. The same principle applies to interaction between colleagues. When your colleague (partner, associate, secretary, etc.) tells you he or she is going to do something and then doesn't do it, how does that make you feel? What impression do you get about that person's value system? Do you trust or respect that person? Lawyers who don't keep their promises struggle to keep clients, and their stress levels are incrementally higher than others.

On the other hand, I have witnessed lawyers who make commitments and stick to them. They create relationships of trust. They create relationships of respect. These lawyers get referrals from their clients for the simple reason that they keep their word. Surprisingly, the quality of legal work can be secondary. What people want most is someone to manage their expectations.

The biggest complaint by clients in disciplinary boards across the country is that their lawyers don't return phone calls. This reminds me of the saying by Woody Allen, "Eighty percent of life is just showing up." What does that mean? To me, it means you can be successful by doing the basic things that most people fail to do. In our Firm, we pursue excellence in communication by returning calls within 24 hours. We also provide project updates regularly, with the goal of never leaving a client wondering if we are working on his or her file. If a client has an open-ended deadline, we make a call to let that client know when to expect to hear from us again. Then, we keep that promise. In most cases, clients rarely care when they actually receive your work product, they simply want to know when to expect it. Proactive communication is a benchmark for doing it right.

PRINCIPLE #4: CARPE DIEM—AND MAKE IT FUN

When I was buying gasoline one weekend, Donna, the young woman behind the cash register, was in an uncharacteristically good mood for someone who works at a convenience store. When I commented on her positive energy, Donna said, "People need to lighten up. It's like . . . man, we're alive."

Donna's attitude reminded me of a movie from 1989, *Dead Poets Society*. In that movie, Robin Williams's character asks his students to focus on the idea of *carpe diem*, which means, "seize the day." A more literal translation of *carpe diem* is "enjoy the day" or "pluck the day (as it is ripe)." My interpretation of the story is that we should all live life to the fullest, enjoying every moment, that there is tremendous value in "right now," and that we should never squander the gift of opportunity. *Carpe diem* is more of an attitude, a mindset, than an exercise.

When I was a young litigation associate at Reed Smith Shaw & McClay (now known as Reed Smith) in the mid-90s, I was working with some of the smartest people and best lawyers I have ever come across. I was involved in many high-level cases getting great experience, and most of the time it was fun—difficult, but fun. One of the partners there, who was in charge of a lot of litigation and responsible for the work of many associates, used to say in stressful situations, "Are we still having fun? When it stops being fun, it is time to do something else."

I believe that partner was being sarcastic because the atmosphere with him in the room was not one of fun and positive energy; it was the exact opposite. Perhaps I was naïve, but I felt the serious environment was purposefully stressful, with the pressure to perform without error associated with every task. That partner was not nurturing and did little to manage expectations. No one seriously spoke about making it fun or about finding pleasure and satisfaction in what we were doing.

At times, the environment working with this partner and his team was intimidating, and, though very unusual, you could find yourself being screamed at if you did not know something or do something as expected. Certainly, the partners were under a great deal of pressure and, as associates, we were simply on the wrong end of someone's stress. At the same time, the associates were all billing 60 hours or more a week, travelling a lot, not sleeping or seeing our families, and gaining weight at an amazing rate. Even the junior partners were intimidated, stressed out, and extremely difficult to deal with. At times, working there was not a lot of fun.

Perhaps that partner was trying to weed out the weak. Maybe that was his way of saying, "If you can't handle it, get out." I don't agree with that. Rather, I believe his sarcasm was his leadership style and his way of thoughtlessly trying to motivate us. Was it an acceptable leadership technique back then? Perhaps. But experience has taught us that such techniques are ineffective today. Leadership training and acceptable office culture have come a long way since then.

To follow the *carpe diem* principle, first, find meaning in your work. Find the satisfaction. Appreciate the value you are bringing by the impact you are making in the life of a person or the success of a business. This is a mindset you can choose. You can choose to be positive about the work you are doing, or you can complain and be miserable. It's up to you.

Second, find balance. Balance is the intersection of striving to be great and enjoying the day. There is no reason you can't work hard and play hard, too. When you are busy, be busy. Get your hours in, but be light-spirited about it when you can. After staying at it for some period, stop in a colleague's office and share something fun that you are working on.

WORDS TO LIVE BY

When I was a teenager, I had a poster on the wall in my bedroom with a picture of someone diving off a cliff. It read, "You only live once, but if you live right, once is enough." Our work as lawyers is a small part of who we are, but it is an important part. It shapes us, and the way we engage with others shapes our lives together. Life is now. Our work as lawyers is now. We should all take a moment every day and remember that today is a great day to be alive. Believe the day to be great, and it will be great.

Interestingly, one day I noticed a poster on our 16-year-old daughter's wall. Her poster quoted Mae West saying, "You only live once, but if you do it right, once is enough."

I asked Katie, "What does that saying mean to you?"

She answered, "That's my life motto."

"Where did you find it?" I asked.

Katie answered casually, "Oh, I just read it somewhere."

How amazing that I had chosen the same motto some 35 years earlier when I was a teenager. Katie and I had never had a conversation about it before. I believe the motto today as much as I ever did.

PRINCIPLE #5: MAKE FRIENDS ALONG THE WAY

Forget the old adage that you should never do business with family or friends. The path to success is in the opposite direction.

Why shouldn't you do business with family or friends? Wouldn't you work harder for a family member or a friend? Are they people you are less likely to take advantage of? My first mentor was a Pittsburgh tycoon who worked at Reed Smith for over 60 years. He would say, "Every client is a friend, and every friend is a client." I've decided to make this a way of life. Your relationships with other people—whether professional, private, personal, or family—make up the building blocks of your network. When you build solid relationships with these people, they will give you business. They will help you meet new people. Their friends will become your friends. Their clients will become your clients.

Now, let's be clear: For this attitude to work for you, you have to commit to your relationships. You *cannot ever* be the person who uses a relationship to give yourself a pass so that you can slack off. If you do, this attitude and strategy is not for you. But if you commit to working extra hard for a friend or a family member and you treat all of your clients the same, you are heading down the right path.

Never forget this truth: People do business with people they *know, like, enjoy,* and *trust*. It takes effort to develop these kinds of relationships, but it's possible if you put in the effort.

Of course, many lawyers try to get business from people without investing much. Those lawyers tend to be average. This book is about how to be better than average—to build a large book of business and a life that is rich with meaning and fun. Life is fleeting, and the best of life is mostly about the relationships you make along the way. Trying to build a relationship-based business without personal relationships will lead to shallow, lonely encounters and an unfulfilling career.

Once, when asked to define the meaning of life, I responded that the meaning of life is sharing life experiences with someone whose company you enjoy without speaking. Every one of my friends is my client—or maybe every one of my clients is my friend. Either way, I've had some tremendous experiences with these people over the 16 plus years I've had my own firm. My wife and kids often host or participate in activities with clients. Friendship with clients is a way of life for me and my family. I would not trade the relationships for anything. Along the way, I've built a multimillion-dollar book of business. You can too.

PRINCIPLE #6: COMMIT TO COURAGE AND RISK

Don't let the fear of rejection hold you back. When I was a senior in high school, I wanted to go to the prom. I didn't have a steady girlfriend, so I had to ask a friend. The first several girls I asked said no. One day between classes, I told my buddy that I was going to ask the next girl that came around the corner in the hallway. Well, I got a date to the prom. It took a few tries, but I did get a date.

It seems to me that building a book of business is a lot like dating. Whether a man or a woman, if you had let your first rejection keep you from ever risking interest in someone else, you would have never gone on another date. Sometimes you must ask a lot of people before you get a date to the prom. How you handle this situation depends on how badly you want to go to the prom. If you want to attend badly enough, you keep asking until you get a date. The same is true with finding and getting clients.

Babe Ruth said, "Don't let the fear of striking out keep you from playing the game." Building a book of business is no different from playing baseball. You will have many at bats; you will strike out a lot; but you will also hit some singles and doubles. You may even get an occasional triple or home run. If you want to build a book of business over $1 million, you will have to accept the fact that you are going to be told no—a lot.

But something odd will occur along the way. You will find that the more confidence you get, the more likely people are to say yes. That goes for the bar scene as well as for building a book of business. Be brave. Have confidence—even if you have to fake it at first. After some time, your success will give you more confidence; your confidence will become more natural, and that, in and of itself, will make you feel great. Consequently, you will exude even more confidence. If you exude confidence, people will want to be around you. People will want you to be on their team. If you exude confidence, people will want you to represent them. If your client has to be in a foxhole, you want that client to think of you at his or her side.

PRINCIPLE #7: CULTIVATE POSITIVE ENERGY

Positive energy, like confidence, is contagious. No one is best friends with the Debbie Downer in the group. In fact, her relationships rarely last long. When is the last time you said, "I feel like being sad; I think I will give Debbie a call?" When you display a fun, positive attitude, people will want to be around you. Potential clients will find your energy contagious and seek you out. They will like you and want to do business with you. You will find that they will begin to invite you to their affairs and events. When that happens, you know you are doing it right.

Hank, a good friend and client, has one of the most upbeat personalities I know. He fills the room with his laugh. When asked how he is doing, he always replies, "Outstanding."

A few years ago, Hank's wife was diagnosed with cancer, operated on, and went into remission. At roughly the same time, Hank's partners forced him to sell his company in a transaction that was not financially profitable for Hank. In fact, Hank had to find a job shortly after the closing to support his nonworking wife and four daughters.

Shortly after the closing, his wife's cancer came back. Hank is currently taking her to the hospital every Monday for a combination cocktail of chemotherapy and radiation. You would never know it. I called him when I heard the news and asked how he was doing. Hank replied, "Outstanding!"

Despite extreme adversity, Hank is back on his feet professionally, and he remains positive personally. He is at the top of the sales team for the company for which he currently works. He is making great money and talking about starting a new business. Hank's positivity is a key ingredient that keeps him resilient and successful in his life's journey.

Building a book of business is a journey with twists, turns, and challenges. The adage I mentioned earlier is worth repeating: the true mettle of a person is revealed not by how that person acts when things are going well, but by how he or she acts when things are going badly.

The behaviors you read about in the following chapters are strategies and tactics. If you are disciplined in performing these behaviors, you will get results. You won't necessarily get million-dollar results, however, unless you make the principles discussed in this chapter a way of life, the foundation for your attitude and perspective. Your attitude is your personality. Your attitude is the foundation upon which you build relationships. In short, the right attitude is the synergy that transforms your business from one that provides transactions to one that provides experiences between a trusted advisor and friends. When you reach that level, your business will take off.

Law is not a 9:00 to 5:00 job or profession. If you are part of the microwave generation that wants immediate success, you can stop reading, because this book is not for you. To build an above-average law practice, you'll need to:

- Embrace hard work

- Pursue excellence

- Commit to keeping your word

- *Carpe diem*—and make it fun

- Make friends along the way

- Commit to courage and risk

- Cultivate positive energy

Living according to these attitudes doesn't come easily. It is not a gift of nature. It is not a personality trait. It is a decision—a way of life. You must *decide* that you want what results from living this way. It is a lot like being in love and staying married. After the honeymoon period is over, many people break up. It is often said that love is a decision. I am not sure about that. I think what they mean is that love is a decision to live a certain way and to stay together. Love may be a feeling, and the *decision* is to stay in the relationship. In the same way, dedicating yourself to building a $1 million book of business is a decision on a way of life you must make if you want to succeed.

If you are willing to embrace these attitudes, you have what it takes to build an above-average law practice. If you want to know about the behaviors these attitudes support, keep reading!

CHAPTER 3

DEVELOP A
CLEAR FOCUS AND DIRECTION

DENTISTS HAVE CONVINCED PEOPLE that they need to come for a checkup every six months. Congress drums up repeat business for accountants by making it nearly impossible for Americans to complete their tax returns without professional help. Semiannual and annual recurring revenue can be foundational to a successful professional practice. How can lawyers build foundations for their own practices?

CHOOSE A STRATEGIC NICHE—WHAT YOU DO

Business lawyers have recurring revenue similar to what dentists and accountants enjoy. Most businesses continue to have needs requiring guidance and counsel over time. Obtaining recurring revenue is more difficult for divorce lawyers, personal injury lawyers, and criminal defense lawyers, because typically those clients are "one and done." If you practice in those areas, try to figure out a way to continue to add value to the relationship you created so that you get recurring revenue.

Our firm, The Lynch Law Group, is a full-service business law firm that represents regional and national clients as advisors and advocates in Pennsylvania and neighboring states. We work hard to establish and maintain a reputation that stretches beyond legal transactions. We aim to be trusted legal and strategic advisors to companies and individuals in helping them achieve their business objectives. We differentiate ourselves with the following mission:

> The mission of The Lynch Law Group is to help clients achieve their goals by providing high-quality, ethically sound legal counsel and strategic advice. We work with clients to understand their objectives, resolve current issues, and proactively anticipate and prevent future problems. We are committed to delivering efficient and cost-effective legal services with a focus on communication, responsiveness, and attention to detail.

Business law has the advantage of naturally recurring revenue, but it may not be for you. Choose an area of legal practice that you are passionate about, then, regardless of your area of practice, stay focused. Don't dilute your model by trying to be everything to everyone. Choose an area and do it well.

Defining your niche includes defining your ideal client—and your bad-fit client. Create a profile of the person who has awareness of the need and the willingness to pay for your services. Figure out where you can connect with that person—at specific associations, networking events, social events, conventions, or trade shows. When you have a clear picture of your ideal client, you are more likely to spend your networking and marketing resources productively, rather than chasing dead ends or bad-fit clients. Bad-fit clients are difficult to define, but you will know them when you see them. Your "spidey" senses will go off; trust your instincts and stay away. There will be more on this topic in the chapter on networking.

If someone on my team meets someone who needs a divorce or a personal injury lawyer, I urge the team member to refer the case out. Engaging in a practice where you are a generalist will never earn you the reputation of being the best at what you do. Don't dabble. If you are a family lawyer, don't take on personal injury cases. If you are a bankruptcy lawyer, don't do white-collar crime. If you focus on insurance defense, don't dabble in business law. The time you spend dabbling is time away from developing your client base and developing your reputation as the go-to lawyer in your area of focus.

PRACTICE AS YOU INTEND TO PLAY: THE "HOW" OF YOUR BUSINESS

I mentioned earlier that our son, Danny, has a goal to play college baseball. Danny loves the sport, and I love spending time with Danny as he practices something he enjoys so much. When he was an early teen, many times when we practiced, Danny would slip into showboating, fielding a ball in a half-assed manner, or jogging to make a play without much intensity or effort. I have told him for years, "You will play how you practice."

Athletes develop habits and fall into routines. Science has proven the power of muscle memory. I am convinced that young athletes who don't practice in a manner exemplifying the highest standards of play will find themselves exemplifying those same *low standards* in a game.

In the book *Outliers*, Malcolm Gladwell espouses that it takes 10,000 hours to become an expert in any field. If that is true, and if muscle memory is true, if you spend your 10,000 hours practicing your craft in a manner that does not execute the correct form, you will be training your body and mind to do it poorly or wrong, and certainly not to the level to which you are aspiring.

This principle holds true in the practice of law. If you want to build a book of business that is better than average, you must spend 10,000 hours developing the routines, habits, and skills to be better than average.

This book is not about how to do great legal work. You already know how to do that. This book is about committing to a way of life. Discipline yourself. Commit yourself to the principles outlined in Chapter 2 of this book. Everything you do should be with these principles in mind. In short, live your life according to them. This will give you the foundation to execute and perform the behaviors outlined in this book.

Develop a short-term plan that will help you develop the habits and routines necessary to give you the foundation to live by these principles. Your short-term plan can be part of your longer-term plan so that when you are done, you will have the foundation to be the person that exemplifies the principles in this book.

LEARN A LESSON FROM HISTORY

As a young man, Benjamin Franklin set a goal to become morally perfect. He enumerated a list of virtues that he wished to master, thinking this plan would lead him to a life without fault. Franklin soon realized that pursuing moral perfection was not only an arduous project but that it would prove impossible. It is still worth contemplating Franklin's approach to life. No one can argue with the accomplishments of this American hero. It is important to note the incredible discipline that was the foundation of Franklin's life.

Franklin named 13 virtues he wished to obtain and provided a short definition for each. Franklin wanted to create habits to achieve all the virtues (and avoid associated faults), but he came to realize that he couldn't concentrate on all the virtues at the same time. Franklin made a book, including a single page for each virtue, to help him master the virtues one at a time. Then Franklin devoted a week to concentrate on each virtue, and repeated the exercise, constantly working on improving his character and habits.

> ### BEN FRANKLIN ON HIS 13 VIRTUES
> I included under Thirteen Names of Virtues all that at that time occurr'd to me as necessary or desirable, and annex'd to each a short Precept, which fully express'd the Extent I gave to its Meaning.

These Names of Virtues with their Precepts were

1.   TEMPERANCE.
Eat not to Dullness.
Drink not to Elevation.

2.   SILENCE.
Speak not but what may benefit others or yourself.
Avoid trifling Conversation.

3.   ORDER.
Let all your Things have their Places. Let each Part of your Business have its Time.

4.   RESOLUTION.
Resolve to perform what you ought. Perform without fail what you resolve.

5.   FRUGALITY.
Make no Expense but to do good to others or yourself: i.e. Waste nothing.

6.   INDUSTRY.
Lose no Time. Be always employ'd in something useful. Cut off all unnecessary Actions.

7.   SINCERITY.
Use no hurtful Deceit.
Think innocently and justly; and, if you speak, speak accordingly.

8.   JUSTICE.
Wrong none, by doing Injuries or omitting the Benefits that are your Duty.

9.   MODERATION.
Avoid Extreams. Forbear resenting Injuries so much as you think they deserve.

10. CLEANLINESS.
Tolerate no Uncleanness in Body, Cloaths or Habitation.

11. TRANQUILITY.
Be not disturbed at Trifles, or at Accidents common or unavoidable.

12. CHASTITY.
Rarely use Venery but for Health or Offspring; Never to Dullness, Weakness, or the Injury of your own or another's Peace or Reputation.

13. HUMILITY.
Imitate Jesus and Socrates.

If Benjamin Franklin seems outdated and irrelevant to you, think again. You can't expect to develop an extraordinary law practice with ordinary behavior. The key ingredients are clarity and discipline.

The following chapters will outline behaviors and practices that lead to success—if you perform them consistently, day after day, month after month, year after year. In and of themselves, the behaviors aren't surprising or even difficult. The difficulty comes on the multiple days you are down, bored, lazy, dejected, and busy. On those days, you need to draw on your habits and the foundation you have built for yourself.

If you approach these attitudes with the commitment Franklin gave to his virtues, you'll find you will soon have developed the way of life for yourself that will serve as the foundation upon which you will build your business and upon which you evolve as a human being. You will find that this foundation serves not only the business development aspect of your law business, but it will serve you in the practice of law itself and in other areas of your life from your introspection (self-reflection and inner confidence) to your relationships with others. Before you know it, you will have your clients' respect, and your reputation will precede you. You will get referrals from clients, business acquaintances, and other service providers. For business lawyers, many of the referrals will come from accountants, financial planners, business brokers, insurance agents, and bankers. For personal injury lawyers, referrals will come from physical therapists, doctors, and chiropractors. For family lawyers, they will come from pastors, psychologists, and therapists. You will soon see the results as your client base grows and referrals begin to come from people you don't even know.

DIG DEEP TO UNDERSTAND AND COMMUNICATE "WHY" YOU ARE IN BUSINESS

Simon Sinek popularized a model, known as the golden circle, which describes how leaders inspire and innovators succeed in the marketplace. According to Sinek, organizations that market "products" or "services" are lacking what is needed to inspire loyalty from customers. Such companies will always be average or below.

According to Sinek, when we tell potential clients "what" we offer (product and service descriptions), they will respond in a less than enthusiastic way. When we tell them "how" we go about providing what we offer, we will get pretty much the same low-key response. The "how" typically includes features, benefits, and that unique selling proposition we've been taught to define.

However, when we tell potential clients "why" we do what we do—what beliefs inspire and energize us—we will attract people and have the opportunity to build mutually loyal relationships. The "why" describes our passion, our vision, and the reason we get out of bed in the morning. The "why" is what makes us unique at the core of things.

Here's a stab at how we might understand Sinek's model in relation to a law practice:

- If you say to a potential client, "Our firm can provide the best legal analysis and documentation you need to run your business," you have provided the "what." Boring.

- If you say that your office is uniquely qualified and uses only cutting-edge technology, you have provided the "how" of what you do. Also boring.

- If you say that your firm exists to provide solid business advice and timely action so executives are free to do what they do best, which is run their businesses, and that you love helping businesses succeed, you have provided the "why." Compelling.

The problem with focusing on "what" or "how" is that they both appeal to reason. People don't make buying decisions based on reason. Like it or not, people make buying decisions with the emotional or limbic portions of their brains. According to Sinek, this is a biological reality. You don't have to like it, but you can't escape it.

If you want an above-average practice, you need to get beyond the idea that legal services are transactions. Better-than-average business lawyers are business advisors who happen to manage transactions. And business advisors have relationships with their clients. They are perceived as trusted and valued resources, even team members and friends. Better-than-average personal injury lawyers connect with their clients in a way that makes them trusted advisors on financial issues for life. Better-than-average family lawyers get requests for advice on a host of family relationship and child-rearing issues well after the divorce is finalized.

An important step in creating a "why-oriented" culture for your firm is to invest energy in developing an authentic mission, vision, and values statement. Of course, most firms have such a statement, and it often is simply an academic exercise resulting in a plaque collecting dust on a wall.

As you can see from the illustration below, we've stretched beyond our mission, vision, and values statement to create a Venn diagram with client satisfaction at the center of everything we are and do. The diagram is a four-leaf clover that describes who we are as a firm, what we do, how we do it, and—most important—why we do it. Other firms use the equivalent of a three-leaf clover in their sales efforts. Following Sinek's findings, we focus on the fourth leaf—the why. If you want to build an above-average book of business, you need to focus on the "why" as well.

Who We Are · **What We Do**

CLIENT SATISFACTION

Professional Satisfaction

Personal Satisfaction

How We Do It · **Why LLG?**

Who We Are

We are a team of talented and skilled business lawyers. Individually, we bring deep experience in each of the various aspects of business law. Collectively, we function as the outsourced legal department for small to midsize companies, providing dedicated advice and creative solutions to help them achieve their business objectives.

What We Do

We combine real-world business experience with broad legal experience to develop business strategies and solutions to our clients' complex matters and problems. We provide the leadership and support necessary to move issues to resolution to the best advantage of the client. We answer clients' legal questions and business questions.

How We Do It

We use the latest technology to maximize efficiency, productivity and profitability, and client service. We set and uphold Best Practice Standards. We make decisions based on integrity and ethics. We put client satisfaction as the number one focus. We strive for excellence in all endeavors, large and small.

Why LLG

Clients choose LLG because: First, we listen, and then we deliver. We earn and retain the confidence of our clients by gaining a thorough understanding of their objectives and then delivering a unique legal services experience that gives them a sense of empowerment and control by jointly agreeing on expectations with regard to cost, time, and outcome. We proactively communicate progress and setbacks and seek to ensure each client understands and fully expects the results they receive and the fees they incur.

MISSION VISION VALUES

MISSION

The mission of The Lynch Law Group is to help clients achieve their goals by providing high quality, ethically sound legal counsel and strategic advice. We work with clients to understand their objectives, resolve current issues, and proactively anticipate and prevent future problems. We are committed to delivering efficient and cost effective legal services with a focus on communication, responsiveness, and attention to detail.

VISION

Our vision is to be the elite boutique business law firm in Western Pennsylvania. We will continue to expand the depth of our practice groups, as well as add new groups, in order to provide clients a broad range of quality services. We will grow our legal team by selectively adding attorneys who can bring to the table a new and diverse approach to client satisfaction. We will grow our support team by adding dedicated, personable, and skilled professionals who can enhance our Firm. The Lynch Law Group will be recognized as the firm with which businesses desire to associate, because of our consistent, proficient lawyers and staff who deliver an exceptional experience in legal services. We endeavor to build our Firm's reputation by satisfying each of our client's needs—one client and one successful outcome at a time.

VALUES

Our core values guide the way we interact with our clients and with each other. They are the standard to which we are accountable in all situations.

We value **INTEGRITY** in all aspects of our work and our lives and are dedicated to maintaining the highest moral standards in our decisions, actions, and communications.

We value **INNOVATION** and continually challenge our-selves to learn and grow. We welcome ideas and pursue changes that will enhance our Firm and the service we provide to our clients.

We value **TEAMWORK AND COLLABORATION** and believe the synergy of our combined individual contribu-tions will elevate the success we achieve for our clients and our Firm.

We value **COMMUNICATION** and understand it is of paramount importance to our success as a Firm. We are com-mitted to timely, responsive, honest, and respectful communi-cation with our clients and with each other.

We value **RESPONSIBILITY** to our clients by manag-ing budgets, reducing extraneous costs, adding value, and meeting their needs completely. We value responsibility to each other to reduce unnecessary costs, work expeditiously and productively, and at all times uphold the image of the Firm.

We value the **PURSUIT OF EXCELLENCE** and be-lieve that in striving for excellence we will not only find suc-cess as a Firm, but fulfillment as individuals.

Mudroom Wisdom

In an effort to inspire our kids, there is a sign in our home hanging above the mudroom as you enter from the kitchen, which our kids walk under multiple times a day. It says:

Watch your thoughts, they become your words;
Watch your words, they become your actions;
Watch your actions, they become your habits;
Watch your habits, they become your character;
Watch your character, it becomes your destiny!

CHAPTER 4

SET GOALS AND HOLD YOURSELF ACCOUNTABLE

CHALLENGES CAN BRING OUT THE BEST (and sometimes, the worst) in people. I have always been a big believer in setting goals. Goals keep you driven. Goals keep you focused. Goal setting is similar to making plans; without a plan, you never know where you are going and when you will get there.

All of us set long-term goals when we were young. We may not have thought we were setting goals, but we were. We set a goal to graduate from college. We set a goal to buy a house. We may have set a goal to get a particular job. Then we performed certain behaviors—executed certain tasks—to accomplish these goals.

If you want to build an above-average book of business, you must set goals for yourself. You must force yourself to make these goals part of your daily life, things you work toward day in and day out. You must approach your business as you would a marathon rather than a sprint.

I have done four marathons in my life (Pittsburgh twice, Erie, and Anchorage). In doing so, I encountered some incredible overachievers. These people get up at 3:45 in the morning to complete their 15-mile run before their kids get up and they have to start their "normal" day. Marathon runners make goal setting and training a way of life. That is how they are able to accomplish so much more than average people.

Of course, people aspiring to run a marathon don't start with 15-mile runs. They start with short runs and condition themselves for longer runs. They make a training plan that extends over months. Then they follow the plan step-by-step. To use the old adage, they eat the elephant one bite at a time.

Can you learn to be a goal-oriented person, or are you simply wired one way or another? You might not be able to change how you are wired, but you certainly can discipline yourself to achieve your goals. You can make setting and achieving goals a habit, even if you don't like it.

At our Firm, we set yearly professional goals that center on being better lawyers and building a book of business. For example, in order to become better lawyers, we know that we have to attend educational events, keep up with our Continuing Legal Education (CLE) requirements, and continually expose ourselves to new developments in the law.

To grow a book of business, we have to continually meet new people and have meaningful conversations with them. The challenge is to ensure we don't get caught up in activities that don't lead to the results we want. We use the following process to make sure that we reach our goals:

1. Clearly define the result we want to achieve
    Example:
    - Get four new clients per month

2. Develop strategies or major approaches that are likely to lead to the desired result
    Examples:
    - Attend events that are attended by people you need to meet

    - Attend networking meetings

    - Build and sustain a network of referral sources

3. Identify specific behaviors that will support the strategies and predict how often you will have to perform the behaviors to meet your goal

    Examples:

    • Attend two networking meetings per month

    • Collect 10 relevant business cards at each networking event

    • Follow up with potential clients or referral sources from networking events by phone or email within 72 hours

    • Meet four potential clients or referral sources for breakfast, lunch, or cocktails per month

    • Attend a monthly referral group

4. Commit to accountability

    • Establish an accountability relationship with a peer within the firm

    • Meet regularly with your accountability partner, per your agreement—weekly or biweekly

5. Measure the results and adjust accordingly

See the visual of this process, which I call the LLG Ladder of Success, on the following page.

THE LLG LADDER OF SUCCESS

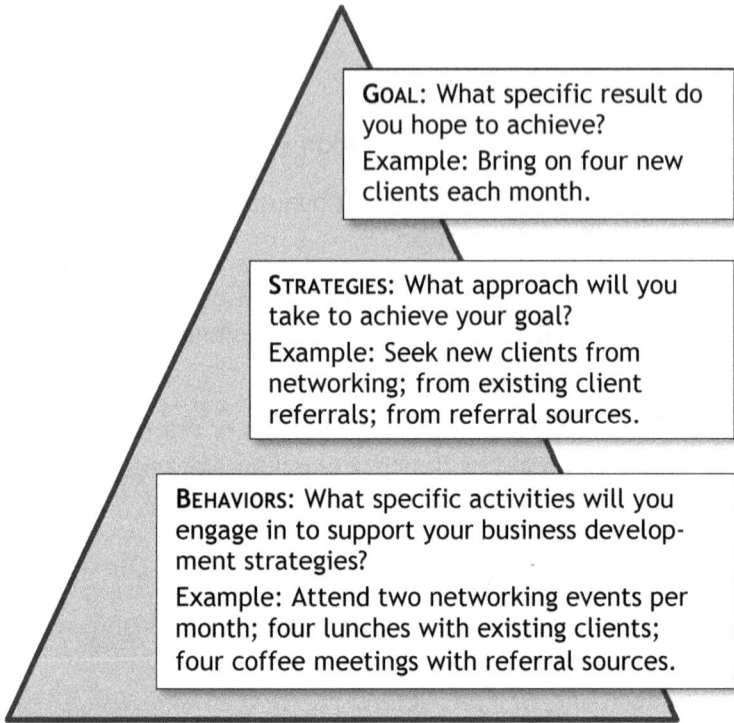

GOAL: What specific result do you hope to achieve?
Example: Bring on four new clients each month.

STRATEGIES: What approach will you take to achieve your goal?
Example: Seek new clients from networking; from existing client referrals; from referral sources.

BEHAVIORS: What specific activities will you engage in to support your business development strategies?
Example: Attend two networking events per month; four lunches with existing clients; four coffee meetings with referral sources.

QUESTIONS TO ASK

1. What is my goal? (number of clients, additional revenue, retained clients, etc.)
2. Where will I look to achieve this goal? What major strategies can I do to achieve this goal?
3. What specific behaviors will I practice for each strategy I identify to achieve my goal?
4. How will I measure these behaviors? Over what period of time? How will I hold myself accountable?

This process is important for several reasons. For starters, it allows us to eat our elephant one bite at a time. It also allows us to focus on things we can control rather than things we cannot.

We can't make anyone become our client, but we can devise strategies to increase the likelihood that we will get clients. We can identify and perform behaviors that support these strategies. These behaviors are known as key-performance indicators or KPIs.

Our goal, as stated above, is to get four new clients a month. A behavior that we know can help us achieve this goal is to meet potential clients or referral sources for first-time appointments (FTAs). That behavior becomes a KPI—and we set a goal to have at least eight FTAs a month. We predict that having eight FTAs each month will contribute significantly to the desired result. Each month, we measure our performance of this KPI—because this is a behavior we can control.

Of course, in order to achieve this KPI, we need a way to meet potential clients and referral sources. In our Firm, we set goals to attend events that lead to FTAs, and we measure our performance against the goals. We also set goals for the FTAs themselves. As business lawyers, we know that attending networking events and meeting referral sources, like bankers, accountants, and financial advisors, lead to FTAs. For lawyers in other specialties, the referral sources and type of networking events will be different. For example, lawyers in a family practice will want to meet other lawyers, marriage counselors, therapists, and spiritual professionals. Personal injury lawyers will want to meet physical therapists, doctors, and other healthcare workers.

In our Firm, experience tells us that attending two appropriate networking meetings per month will lead to the FTAs we want. This becomes a KPI we can measure.

Each of the behaviors we undertake to land four new clients a month is a KPI. With this goal-setting process, each step is aligned with the others, increasing chances of success. When we get to the behavioral level, we can write down our behavioral goals and measure progress against the standards we have set.

Here's how the process works for me: My personal goal is to generate $1 million in business per year. Because I measure my performance, I know from the past that I'll need to serve roughly 200 clients in a year to achieve this goal. Forty percent of those clients will provide above $10,000 of business in a given year, and 60 percent will provide less than $10,000. However, because not all clients need my services each year, I need a base of 1,000 clients to get 200 to engage my services in any given year. And every year, my base of 1,000 clients has some attrition, for any number of reasons. Based on this analysis, I know that I need roughly 40 new clients a year to achieve my goal of $1 million. How do I eat this elephant one bite at a time?

I eat my personal elephant one bite at a time with these behavioral goals: Attend one networking meeting a week and have 10 FTAs a month. With these behaviors, I am able to close roughly three or four new clients a month and achieve my goal of $1 million in business annually.

The lawyers who work with me haven't yet achieved $1 million in business, but they know the KPIs that will get them there. Each individual sets SMART goals (see the explanation below), and we have accountability partners. The accountability partners meet every week or so to ensure members are on track in accomplishing their goals.

SMART GOALS INCREASE YOUR CHANCES FOR SUCCESS

To increase our chances of meeting our goals at The Lynch Law Group, we use SMART goals. The SMART goal formula was first introduced by George T. Doran in the November 1981 issue of *Management Review*. Today, people vary somewhat in how they designate the letters of the acronym. In our Firm, goals must be Specific, Measurable, Achievable, Relevant, and Timely.

Typically, when people set goals, their goals are vague or ambiguous. Perhaps people do this subconsciously so they have some wiggle room when deciding whether they achieved their goal. An important aspect about setting goals in a workplace environment is to draft them in such a way so as to avoid ever having to argue about whether a goal was achieved. For that reason, when we are discussing goal setting at our Firm, I spend a lot of time talking about making sure that a goal is measurable and specific. For example, the goal to "attend networking meetings regularly" sounds nice, but it can be interpreted in different ways. We can't hold each other accountable for such a goal. We may disagree regarding what "regularly" means. We might also disagree with what types of networking events are appropriate.

The goal becomes measurable and specific if we change the goal to "attend four business-related networking events each month." At the end of the year, there will be no doubt about whether that goal was achieved. It either was or it wasn't.

Within our Firm, we use charts like the following to measure and communicate our progress.

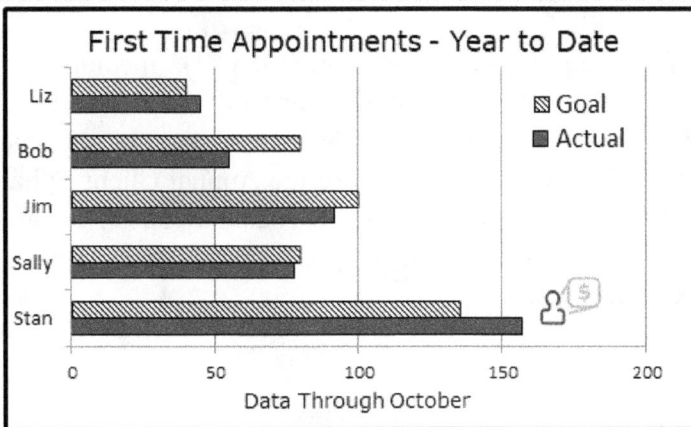

First Time Appointments - Year to Date

Data Through October

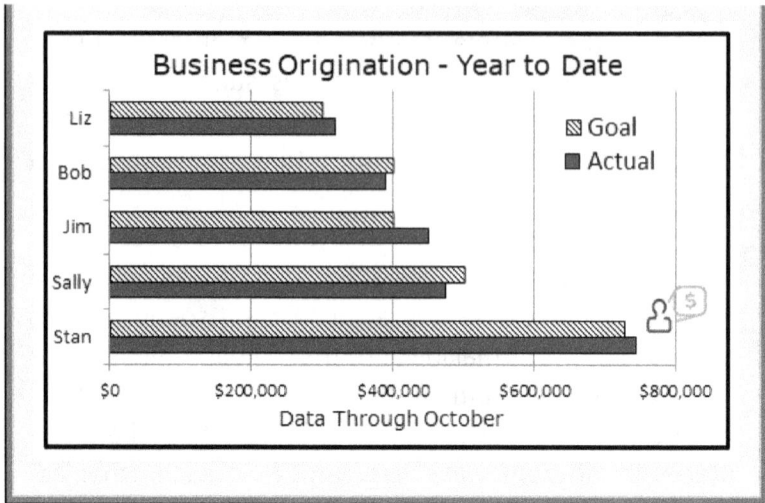

It is easy to let yourself off the hook when you fail to do something you set your mind to do. Being accountable to another person is another story altogether. This is why many of us pay $90 a month to belong to a gym when we have weights and a treadmill in the basement or workout room. It's why we join Weight Watchers®, where we agree to show up and weigh in once a week, when we know the formula to losing weight is to eat less and work out more. But the secret is accountability. Sharing your goals with a boss, colleague (we call them accountability partners), or spouse helps with accountability.

We should each have large (annual), medium (semi-annual), and small (every 30 days or less) goals. This helps us to look at the big picture while managing time and energy productively. At our firm, we use the Annual Client Enhancement Plan to help us break annual goals into specific manageable pieces. Whatever your goals, remember to use the SMART formula.

Annual Client Enhancement Plan

What is my revenue goal?

What is my average revenue per client?

How many new clients do I need to hit my goal?

What is my closing ratio?

How many first-time appointments (FTAs) will I need?

In order to hit my goal, how many potential clients will I need to meet?

How often will I meet with my referral sources?

How many networking events will I need to attend?

How often will I touch base with existing clients?

Set goals for the KPIs I've outlined above, but set other goals as well. For example, one year you might set a goal to attend a sales training course. You might also set a goal for your behavior at networking events so that you do more than show up.

You might set a goal to host a networking event or secure an invitation to be a featured speaker at a function. Either of these roles will change the dynamic and make following up for that FTA easier.

Set stretch goals by showing up in new places and meeting new people. Also set goals that stretch you to develop new competencies and deepen you as an individual. Set goals to embrace topics and areas of interest that will help you to be a more interesting conversationalist.

As you think about setting goals, focus on what you can control, and hold yourself accountable to control those things. The more you engage in the *activities* that you can control, the more likely you are to get the *results* (referrals) you desire. You can't guarantee the referrals, but you can and must stack the deck. It's all about discipline over time.

There's nothing new in the practice of networking—lawyers have been building relationships this way for years. Make sure that attending networking meetings is one of your top KPIs. Measure your progress, and you'll measure your success.

CHAPTER 5

ESTABLISH A NETWORK

W HEN I STARTED MY OWN PRACTICE in 2002, I knew I needed to meet people, but I did not know how. Having spent the previous 10 years at a mega firm, a start-up company, and a midsize corporation, my business contacts were limited. Someone told me that I needed to network. I am not even sure I knew what the term meant at the time, but now I know there's nothing complicated about it. Networking is simply getting to know other people.

I started making calls and was referred to Richard, an owner of an automobile dealership. When he answered my call, which was a surprise, I attempted to tell Richard why I wanted to meet with him and get to know him. I stumbled over my words and probably sounded like a 12-year-old. Richard quickly let me off the hook, saying, "You want to network. It's okay to say it. Networking isn't a dirty word."

In Chapter 2, I mentioned the Woody Allen quote that claims 80 percent of life is just showing up. When it comes to networking, however, you can't show up just anywhere. It's important to show up in a potential client-rich environment. You also need to show up where your referral sources are.

As a young lawyer, I was advised to get involved with the bar association, which I did enthusiastically. When you are attending bar association events or activities, of course, you are with a bunch of lawyers—many of whom are your competitors. This isn't the best strategy to build an above-average book of business, at least for most lawyers.

Don't get me wrong. Bar associations are important for lawyers. They serve specific functions for the profession. They create a forum for the judges and lawyers to communicate and collaborate, receive training and CLEs, debate current events affecting the profession, and discharge tension in a profession that centers on controversy. And some business models, like those of personal injury lawyers, rely on referrals from other lawyers. If that's true of your business model, it's a good idea to get to know as many different lawyers as you can. Bar associations are referral-rich environments for personal injury lawyers.

I remember attending my first bar association event after I was hired at Reed Smith in 1994. I attended with a midlevel partner who was my boss at the time. He told me the story of an old Pittsburgh lawyer who, 20 years earlier, while walking into a similar event with my boss, rubbed his hands together while saying, "There is money to be made here; see you later."

After I started my own Firm, it did not take me long to learn that my business model required me to get out of the bar association and get into places where the general population hangs out. I also learned that it did not matter what I did to meet people; I just had to do something. Better yet, I had to do multiple things. Business owners and those who know them are everywhere. For a business lawyer, potential client-rich environments are everywhere.

Consider your own potential, client-rich environments. Then pick hobbies, venues, and activities you know you will enjoy.

Here are some examples that might work for you:

- Become active in your local Chamber of Commerce

- Join a country club

- Join a shooting club

- Coach a kids' sports team

- Run for school board

- Become active in your church or synagogue

- Serve on a board

- Join an association

- Join a formal networking group, like BNI (Business Network International)

- Teach a class or CLE

The basic rule is simple: In order to network effectively, put yourself in a position to meet many, many people. Surround yourself with people who hire lawyers or refer lawyers to other people.

Networking can be exhausting, especially in the beginning, but it does pay off. When I first started, I invited and met someone for coffee, lunch, or drinks almost every day. When my accountant saw my financial records, he said there was no way that I had been to Starbucks that many times. I responded that indeed I had been, and I had every receipt to prove it. I can trace a lot of business to some of those early meetings.

Because networking is so important and because we all need to be accountable, we urge all the lawyers in our Firm to set goals and keep track of their FTAs. Of course, we also keep track of business origination. There is a direct correlation between FTAs and originations. The people with the highest number of FTAs have the largest books of business. You may not like this equation, especially if you are an introvert, but it is a rule of the universe.

You might think about it this way: There are two ways to monetize a billable hour in the practice of law. It does not matter whether you bill by the hour or you get a contingency fee. Either you originate the hour of work or you produce it. In other words, you are the one who goes out and gets the work, or you are the one who does the work—or you are both. Always be thinking about the work you are bringing in and the work you are doing. Striking that balance is one of the hardest things we do as lawyers.

Set your annual goals around your originations and the number of hours you want to work, and you will quickly learn that the more you build your network, the more your originations will increase. It is simply a matter of volume and your reputation. The more people who know you are a lawyer, the more people out there who will think of you when they are presented with the need for a lawyer or are in the presence of someone who needs, or is otherwise looking for, a lawyer.

Networking Is Scary, But That Can Work in Your Favor

A good place to meet people is at events advertised as networking events. Attending these can be intimidating because these events are like going to a high school dance—by yourself. Maybe networking events are even worse than dances, because at least at the dance you know your friends will be there.

At a networking event, the whole idea is to meet new people, and everyone is there for the same reason. Even so, the whole experience can bring up feelings of vulnerability and insecurity. I have learned, after years and years of networking, that everyone feels exactly the same way. Everyone is nervous. Everyone feels self-conscious. Once you accept this truth, the event becomes a lot less scary.

At any networking event, you will see a variety of behaviors. If you stand back and observe, you will see the wallflower who is talking to no one; that person is nervous. You will see the bar stool anchor; that person is definitely nervous. You will see the person who globs on to the first person who will talk to him or her—for the entire event. That person is feeling insecure and attaching to someone else makes the person feel better. You will see people in a tight knot, hanging out with people they know. They are too nervous to break away and meet new people. Why do these people even attend the event?

Researcher, popular author, and TED Talk speaker Brené Brown claims that certain situations make everyone feel vulnerable. Any situation in which you might be rejected qualifies. A networking event where you are supposed to meet new people and talk about yourself certainly qualifies.

Once you realize everyone is nervous at networking events, you can use that knowledge to your advantage. Perhaps you can find the courage within yourself to acknowledge to others that such events are nerve wracking. This allows others to admit their own vulnerability. Your simple acknowledgement can break the ice and lead to a great connection. You don't have to be pathetic to be honest. There is nothing wrong with saying something like: Hi, my name is _____. Bang. Ice breaker. And now you are having a conversation.

Another strategy is to take the role of initiator. Walk up to someone, put your hand out first, say hello, and introduce yourself. That is a huge icebreaker, and the other person will be grateful that you made the first move and literally diffused a universally awkward moment.

Taking the initiative also puts you in control. You become a leader. You establish yourself as someone who is more friendly and confident than nervous, no matter how you actually feel. Think of it as a game. An act. Pretend not to be nervous. Trust me, the other person is nervous too—and probably more nervous than you.

By making the first move, you project confidence. That is what people want in a lawyer and any other service professional. You have confidence, you are personable, and you are not easily intimidated. Say something intelligent and you have become—and people will think of you as—the ideal lawyer.

Networking gets easier and easier every time you attend an event. Think of the first few as practice. Like everything else, the more you practice, the better you will get. What is the worst that can happen? You are not going to get physically hurt. Probably no one is even going to be rude to you. You might meet some interesting people. You might even have fun. After a while, meeting new people will become natural to you and networking will lose much of its sinister atmosphere. Even if you never find networking a favorite activity, you can become skilled at it.

Remember, you attend networking events to meet people. Work the room. Don't be a wallflower. Talk to someone for 10 to 15 minutes tops. Then move on. If someone tries to glob onto you, politely say, "It was nice to meet you. Please excuse me. I am going to go say hello to a couple other people." This is completely acceptable. Everyone is there to meet people. You will even reassert yourself as having confidence, because most people accept the "glob on." You will set yourself apart as having the confidence to move away from a secure conversation into one that is less secure. To the person you are talking to, that is scary. You are the ideal lawyer.

STRATEGIES FOR NETWORKING SUCCESS

In today's business world, virtually everyone networks— but very few network effectively. Many people who attend events have nothing at all to show for it. Done correctly, however, networking is the most powerful source for business. Here are some ways to get the most mileage out of this tool.

FOLLOW UP

One of the hardest parts of networking is the follow-up. What good is it to meet someone, shake hands, and have a good conversation if that person forgets you soon afterward? The secret to success is scheduling the next encounter. When you meet a person who seems to be a good potential client or referral source, invite that person for coffee or lunch. You can extend the invitation during the initial conversation or by phone or email within a week. This becomes your FTA.

After you meet someone for the first time (the FTA), assuming there is no need to follow up immediately, get in touch with that person again in 30 to 45 days. The follow-up does not have to be long, although it can be. It can be as simple as an email, a quick call, sending an article, or as detailed as a lunch, dinner, or drinks. That decision will be predicated on who the person is and the role that person plays, or can play, in the development of your network. You are building a relationship. You want that person to get to know you, and you want to get to know that person. The important point is to make yourself top of mind. You want that person to think of you the next time someone asks if he or she knows a good lawyer.

Please remember, any event where you can meet someone new is a networking event. It doesn't have to be called a networking event for it to qualify as one. The social gathering at your kids' school can be a networking event. The boosters meeting can be a networking event. The church council can be a networking event. The book club or country club can be a networking event. The important part for you to remember is that regardless of the type of event, you treat it as a networking event. As you do this, you will see your business grow.

CREATE YOUR OWN REFERRAL GROUP

Attending events that others stage is a somewhat passive approach to networking. An active, supercharged networking tactic is to create your own networking group. Put together a group of service professionals who can help each other meet people and potential clients. In the business sector, you want to include an accountant, a banker, an insurance broker, a financial advisor, and anyone else who calls on decision makers. Imagine how such a group can multiply your referrals—and how you can multiply theirs.

Depending on the focus of your practice, think through who should be in your group. For example, if you are a criminal lawyer, knowing police officers and detectives may be good. If you are a divorce lawyer, knowing priests and marriage counselors may be good. Personal injury lawyers and workers' compensation lawyers want to know doctors, chiropractors, hospital workers, union stewards, and physical therapists. The principle to remember is that you want to associate with people who will be able to introduce you to other referral sources and potential clients. These people will be able to influence the trajectory of your practice and the growth of your book of business.

Invite people into your referral group who are hungry to build their book of business. It does not do any good to have someone who is sitting on his or her book and not working very hard to grow it. Be certain your group is comprised of people who are around the same place in their lives and careers as you. If you have kids, choose people who have kids your kids' ages. You want people who are as desperate as you are to feed their families and put kids through college. Since you are trying to build a relationship with these people, it only makes sense to be situated similarly in life. You will find that you will grow your practices together.

Get your referral group together for an hour every week. Use the time to share referrals and experiences. Go through your calendars and your contacts every week and identify people who would be good for your fellow networking group members to know. They will do the same for you. You will learn from these people, and they will learn from you. These people may become your good friends. Your families may do things together, and you may even go on trips together. Once this happens, there will come a time when you will no longer need the weekly meeting to ensure that you are on the top of mind for everyone in the group.

ASK FOR MEETINGS

People like to help other people. The hard part is our fear, or perhaps embarrassment, of asking for help. Once again, the fear of rejection makes us feel vulnerable. Yet, to succeed, we must get over the fear of asking for things.

First, ask for meetings. When you meet someone at a networking event or by introduction, invite the person to coffee or lunch—and buy. Make it as convenient as possible for the other person.

When I have met someone who expresses a need for a lawyer, I often send an email that goes something like this:

Hey _____:

It was nice to meet you at the networking event the other day. I would love to get together one of these days for coffee or lunch. Naturally, it will give me an opportunity to further introduce myself and my firm to you. Obviously, I want to learn more about you and your business. Typically, after 30 or 40 minutes we will know whether we are a good fit for each other. What do you say? In the meantime, check out *www.lynchlaw-group.com*. That will give you some details about who we are, what we do and how we do it. It will also tell you way more than you will ever want to know about me and my background.

When I meet someone who doesn't need a lawyer now, the invitation might go something like this:

Hey _____:

It was nice to meet you at the networking event the other day. I would love to get together to learn more about your business and your success. It sounds like I can learn a thing or two from you. What do you say?

When I meet another service professional who might be a good referral source, the invitation might go something like this:

Hey _____:

It was nice to meet you at the networking event the other day. It seems like we can help each other out. We are both looking to meet the decision makers in small to middle market companies. What do you think about having a coffee to get to know each other and explore how we might be able to work together?

ASK FOR NAMES

When you meet with anyone, always ask the person for the names of at least two people "who would be good for me to meet." Don't end the meeting until you've asked this question.

USE LINKEDIN

LinkedIn is the social media tool of choice for professionals. It is an awesome tool for meeting people who may be potential clients or who may help you find potential clients. It allows you to see the "network" of the people in your "networks." On occasion, I become aware of someone I want to meet, and I use LinkedIn to find someone in my network who knows that person. I then email my contact, acknowledging that I saw that he or she was "LinkedIn" with the person I want to meet, and then ask for an introduction.

There are other avenues of social media that may help you connect with potential clients and referral sources. Facebook is one of them. Technology is expanding at an ever-increasing rate. By the time this book is published, there may be new sites, new apps, and new ways to introduce yourself to people on a professional basis. Find them. Implement them. And then the hard part: use them.

Even very successful people are people. They want to help. Don't be afraid to ask. You can ask for help without appearing needy. Sometimes the person will offer to make a warm introduction with an email, which you should allow them to do. If the person doesn't make this offer, just send your own email introduction. If you get an introduction to a potential client or referral source via email, you can simply replace the first sentence in any of the above with, "It is nice to meet you electronically."

ASK FOR A PROJECT

When you are with a potential client who seems to be having an internal debate about hiring you, make it easy for the person. Suggest that he or she just give you one small project, to see what you are capable of. That way the potential client is not investing in you without a practice run. It will feel like less of a commitment for the potential client, and it gets you in the door. Once in the door, be sure to practice the principles outlined in Chapter 2. That means you say what you are going to do, and then do what you say. Keep every promise you make. Respond as quickly as possible to any inquiries, and return all telephone calls the same business day.

If a potential client already has a lawyer or law firm, never say anything negative about their existing law firm. Compliment your potential client on the prestige of their existing relationship. Then say something like this:

> I never suggest that a potential client abandon the relationship with their existing firm, especially if it is a large law firm. That relationship should be cultivated and nurtured. But maybe there is room for both of us. I have a client who calls me her primary care lawyer. We get all of her day-to-day lawyering, and when she has some-

thing that warrants a specialization we don't offer, she hires the big firm. This client says she does not need a brain surgeon to set a little finger.

MAKE INTRODUCTIONS

A powerful way to ingratiate yourself to someone is to help that person succeed. That means to give a referral. When you give a referral, the other person feels the obligation to give one in return. This is human nature. I have heard it referred to as the guilt bank. If you can't refer a client or a customer, then connect the individual with someone who will be able to help that person in some way.

If you make an introduction that helps the person in some way, you look good. One caveat: Be sure to surround yourself with solid people. Never refer someone you would not use or hire yourself. The worst thing you can do is introduce someone to a professional who does a bad job. Every one of your referrals is a reflection of you.

HONOR YOUR SOURCES

As you meet more and more people and make more and more introductions, you will find yourself in a situation where you have been referred to someone who in turn asks you to refer them to someone else. Resist the urge to refer your network into that relationship.

Networking rule 101 dictates that the person who referred you "owns" the relationship. That means you defer to the person who originally referred you in. Your response should be something like, "Let me check with [person who referred you] and get back to you."

When you go back to the person who referred you, two things will happen. First, the person who referred you will have a new respect for you for deferring to him or her. The person will appreciate that you recognize and respect the relationship between the referring person and the potential client and are letting him or her control that relationship. You have not tried to usurp that friendship or relationship. Second, the person who asked for the referral will gain respect for you for your loyalty. It is a win-win approach.

PRACTICE

There is no way around it. If you want to build an above-average book of business, you will have to get used to networking. So, the question becomes, how do you get proficient at networking? The answer is simple: practice. Put yourself in low-risk situations and practice. Go to chamber events and practice your pitch (I'll help you build your pitch in the next chapter). Go to your local community's networking events and meet people. Go to the church social and the PTA meeting. Keep focused on building the network of people who know you. Meet as many people as you can. Tell your story. Do this repeatedly. You will learn what comes off well and what does not. You will refine your pitch over time.

You cannot screw up. Nothing can go radically wrong. The only bad thing that will happen is that you might believe you could have performed better. So what! That is okay. You will not get hurt. You will not embarrass yourself in some unredeemable way. You might think something you say or do is embarrassing, but so what!

Think of networking as making new friends. Think of it like the first day of college or law school. And remember, at a networking event, other people are there doing the same thing as you. If ever there is a place where you will get a pass, it is at an event designed for people to meet other people. The important thing is to practice extending yourself so that you get comfortable meeting people wherever you happen to be. If you want to have an above-average book of business, you can never meet enough people.

You might also think of networking in terms of dating. Whatever your gender, a good date is when the other person listens to everything you say and hangs on every word. On my first date with my wife, I am pretty sure I did not say a word about myself. I just kept saying "uh huh." I kept asking questions. At the end of the evening, Susan said, "This was so much fun. You are so interesting." The funny part was that I had barely said a word.

So, what does this tell us? Does it mean that my wife is self-absorbed and egocentric? Nothing could be further from the truth. It means Susan was nervous, and I helped her feel comfortable by asking her questions that kept her talking. I found out a lot about her by what she told me, and Susan found out a lot about me by the questions I asked.

Ask follow-up questions. Be surprised. Be enthusiastic. Be positive. Ask more questions. Find common ground and let the other person run with it. People will be put at ease and enjoy you more if you listen and express interest in what they say. Your conversation companion will learn how thorough you are by the details you solicit. You will leave that person with the impression that you are likeable, trustworthy, and someone with whom he or she could work.

Effective networking is essential to building an above-average book of business. There is no way around it, and the time for excuses is long over. Grab your calendar, identify some networking events or opportunities, sign up for something, and get started.

CHAPTER 6

PERFECT YOUR PITCH

HAVING A "PERFECTED PITCH" is an overused phrase that carries so much baggage. First, it sounds so "salesy." Second, it sounds like something someone can get really anxious about. The hype is much ado about nothing.

There are many types of pitches. Sales people talk in terms of the two-minute pitch, also known as the elevator pitch. For the elevator pitch, your description of your services should take no longer than the time it takes to ride up or down in an elevator. (Doesn't that depend on how tall the building is? Or what floor you are getting off?) There is also the beauty contest type of pitch. This pitch is more detailed and is used when you are being interviewed by a potential client who is comparing you to other lawyers or firms. There is the tagline pitch, the question pitch, the email-subject-line pitch, the Twitter pitch, and I have even heard of the Pixar story pitch. Pitch. Pitch. Pitch.

PRACTICE YOUR ANSWERS TO THREE SIMPLE QUESTIONS

Forget the pitch. It is this simple: Answer these three simple questions:

1. What do you do?
2. For whom do you do it?
3. What makes you different?

If you can answer these questions, you have a pitch. The only other factor is how long you have to make your pitch in any given situation. As masters of language, lawyers ought to be able to adjust their thoughts to the time they have to explain those thoughts. If you only have two minutes, you better be able to explain what you do in two minutes. Most lawyers are brevity challenged. Perhaps that is why lawyers often get accused of billing by the word. Although you sometimes need a pitch with more detail than you can make in two minutes, I don't think your explanation of what you do should ever take more than 10 minutes. [Insert your own boring-lawyer story here.]

Here is the point: You need to be able to tell people what you do and tailor it to particular time periods and audiences. And most important, you need to practice.

Lawyers practice for their oral arguments. Business people practice their presentations. Politicians practice their speeches. Actors rehearse their lines. If you were scheduled for an important job interview, wouldn't you practice for that? It may sound a little hokey, but talking with a potential client is a job interview, no matter what type of law you are in. So practice.

Begin by practicing in low-risk settings. At first, that means practicing in front of the mirror. Start with a summary of what you do. This is the two-minute version. The Pixar version, which is a little more detailed, tells your story, but in no longer than 10 minutes. The next step is to record your pitch and listen to it. If you own a smart phone, you have this technology. The next level is to practice in front of your spouse and kids. If you can explain what you do to your spouse and children, you can explain it to anyone.

After you graduate from explaining what you do to your spouse and kids, practice with your referral group. These are the people you meet with regularly, those who have the ability to refer you business.

Once you can give your pitch to other professionals, it is time to go to an event where you will meet people who will ask you what you do for a living, simply to make conversation. Choose a low-risk setting: It could be a dinner party, happy hour, the reception after your kid's chorus concert, or the block party. If the unthinkable happens and no one asks you what you do, turn the tables. Ask them. When you do this, two things will happen. First, you will get to hear how other people describe what they do—or give their pitch. Second, when people are done telling you what they do, they are almost certainly going to ask you what you do.

After you are comfortable talking about what you do in these low-risk settings, it is time to step up your game. Attend a networking event, the country club, or a business affair. Generally speaking, you would never give your 10-minute description of what you do at these events. It is not the right time or place. Resist the urge to go into a lot of detail, even if the person you are talking to seems interested and is asking you probing questions. In that instance, it is appropriate to say something like, "I don't want to bore you with too much talk about business at this event. Why don't we get coffee or lunch one of these days? I would like to learn more about what you do too."

The only difference between the previously mentioned low-risk events and something with higher risk is a *perception* that the stakes are higher. But that is just it—it is a perception. The stakes are not higher. What is the worst that can happen in any case? Every event where you have an occasion to describe what you do to another person (okay, not your spouse and kids) is an opportunity to make a connection that turns into business. You never know who else might be at an event—or who any individual knows. A full-time parent's connections may be as valuable as those of a CEO. It depends on the person.

When attending any type of event, be conscious of your posture and your clothes, as well as of what you eat and drink. Make it your objective to exude confidence. You want your conversation partner to be thinking that you are intelligent, have confidence, that you believe what you say, and that you say it with conviction. Ask smart, probing questions. This will show that you care and are interested in the other person. You want the person to think that if he or she ever needs a lawyer, that lawyer would be just like you.

ADJUST YOUR PITCH TO YOUR CONVERSATION PARTNER

When you meet with a potential client, as opposed to a referral source, talk about what you do in terms of what they do and need. In other words, encourage people to tell you about themselves before you talk about you. In that part of the conversation, you will learn about their business, their needs, and their pain. Ask probing questions, demonstrate your interest in them, show your empathy, and convey a command of the type of law you practice. When it is your turn to give your pitch, tailor your presentation to the other person's needs. If a person is considering bankruptcy, talk about your experience in dealing with similar cases. If you are talking to someone who is contemplating divorce, describe how you have handled similar divorce cases. If you are talking to a business owner, talk about similar companies that you represent. This makes you a subject matter expert in that potential client's eyes.

YOU NEVER KNOW
HOW YOU WILL FIND YOUR NEXT BIG CLIENT

I once had a situation where I was doing a modest estate plan for an older couple. I had no idea who they were. I believe they found me through the church bulletin. As we were wrapping up the execution of the documents, the gentleman told me that he wanted me to meet his sons. It turns out the gentleman had run a business for 40 years and given it to his two boys. The business had 70 employees and was worth around $30,000,000. This business has been a client ever since.

When sales people talk about finding a potential client's pain, they are talking about what keeps that person up at night. What problem is your potential client dealing with that you can solve? Oftentimes you have to ask the same question several different ways to get to the real answer. People don't like to admit that they have a problem. They have to be able to trust you first. Once they trust you, they will tell you everything. Be sure also to talk about the cost of their pain. What is the monetary cost to them of doing nothing? This will put in perspective the value of your service. During a conversation about pain, elicit a commitment from your potential client to deal with the issue. A potential client has to be ready to invest the dollars to solve the problem. Often people will understand their pain, understand the cost, but still be unwilling to deal with it.

BE READY TO EXPLAIN WHAT MAKES YOU DIFFERENT

Many lawyers out there do what you do. Why should the person you are meeting with hire you? A good pitch demonstrates how you are different. What is it about you that is different than most? What is it about the way you conduct your practice that will give the client a better experience than if they hire someone else? A good way to make your case is to tell third-party stories. When a potential client hears about how good you are from someone else's mouth rather than yours, the message is more convincing and credible. I am not suggesting you bring a reference to the meeting. Rather, it goes something like this: "I have a client who says that I . . ." Here you insert something that is relevant to the potential client and unique to you. Make sure the message is different from what the potential client will hear from other lawyers.

In my pitch, I often explain to potential clients that I can function as their primary-care lawyer. In health care, most people have a primary-care physician they consult for normal, everyday health issues. They have a strong ongoing relationship with this physician who knows their history and chronic health concerns. Only when something acute, dangerous, or complicated occurs do people go to specialists like oncologists or orthopedic doctors. For most issues, these doctors are not needed and/or are not cost effective. After all, who would seek to pay oncologist fees to get medicine for poison ivy?

I make the case that business law is a lot like medicine. Businesses need a relationship with a day-to-day lawyer in the same way individuals need a relationship with a primary-care physician. It doesn't make business sense to pay $800 an hour to a specialized firm for day-to-day legal services. I serve as a primary-care lawyer. That's my distinction.

TALK ABOUT MONEY

Talking about money is hard. Most of us were raised in homes where discussions about money were taboo. You may recall getting curious about money and your family's financial situation when you were a teenager. You probably asked your mom and dad how much money they made, and you probably did not get a straight answer. Then there was the discussion about how much your house was worth. Again, not a straight answer.

For most of us, these early experiences represent the beginning of our discomfort talking about money. As lawyers trying to build a book of business, we must rid ourselves of that head trash. You have to talk about the money. If you fail to talk about money, you can be assured there will be a misunderstanding about what you think a particular project or assignment is worth and what the potential client thinks it should cost.

When, and in what detail, you talk about money is important. You don't talk about money at a networking event. And you might not even talk money at an FTA with a potential client unless that potential client has immediate pain and is looking for a solution. If that is the case, or even if you are talking to an existing client, you have to talk about how long the project will take and how much it will cost. Failing to do so will almost certainly come back to haunt you.

Almost all clients have an unrealistic view of how long something takes in our world, and consequently what it should cost. I have been burned by this many times and have learned the lesson repeatedly. It is far better to overestimate what a project will cost and risk losing the client, than to underestimate what it will cost and have to explain to your client why it cost more than you said, or alternatively write off part of your bill. That is why it is so important to manage a client's or potential client's expectations about cost.

In terms of a long-term relationship, candid conversations about money positively affect credibility. Your client has to be able to trust you. If the first experience with you is a misunderstanding about cost, chances are your relationship will be over before it really gets started.

In terms of managing expectations, also talk about timing. When does the client need to hear back from you? What is a reasonable time for you to deliver? As we discussed in an earlier chapter, I have learned that clients generally don't care when you tell them you will get back to them; they simply want to know what to expect. And by all means, keep whatever commitment you make.

Your discussion on timing is similar to your discussion on cost. In this case, avoid the temptation to give yourself a deadline you can't make. For some reason, there is a temptation among lawyers to want to overpromise. We think that a client wants a fast turnaround time, we want to impress them, and we want to serve. This all leads to a tendency to create an unrealistic expectation of when the client will hear back from us. When we fail to deliver on any promise, we create a credibility issue.

Imagine this scenario: You are meeting with a new client on a Friday about a particular project. You are itching to say you will have something to the client by Monday, which is a huge stretch because of all your other commitments. At the very least, you'd have to disappoint your family by working over the weekend. Stop yourself from promising something by Monday. Instead, ask, "Would it be okay if I got back to you on Wednesday?" Absent extraordinary circumstances, Wednesday is likely to be perfectly fine, and it is a time frame you can meet without much trouble.

DON'T TRY TO SET YOURSELF APART WITH PRICE OR QUALITY. SELL VALUE.

Many sales experts say that you should never sell on price or quality. Their point is that when you sell on price, you undercut the value of your service. Besides, it's extremely difficult to make a good living as the lowest cost provider in the law business.

Similarly, when you sell on quality, you are not giving anything that sets you apart from your competitors. Everyone claims high quality, whether they deliver it or not.

I suggest you talk about your successes. Describe how your experiences put you in a unique position to deliver service that will be distinct from your potential clients' other legal experiences. There is a difference between saying that you are the best (everyone is going to say that) and talking about the experience your potential client will have by working with you.

Here's a big difference: Most bad experiences clients have with lawyers is not about the legal work itself. The biggest complaint to most disciplinary boards is that lawyers don't return calls in a timely manner or don't follow up on what they say they are going to do. You can always sell against that.

Your pitch should include promises that you return your telephone calls and emails within the same business day or within 24 hours at the latest. Remember the earlier discussion in Chapter 2 about Woody Allen and 80 percent of life is just showing up? Returning your calls and emails within the same business day or within 24 hours, and keeping your promises, is just showing up. Do that and you are ahead of most lawyers. Of course, you should never promise results, but you should always promise a great experience, which begins with great service. You can promise that you will say what you are going to do, and that you will do what you say. If you have conviction when you make those promises and you keep your word, you are ahead of 80 percent of the lawyers out there.

Pitch isn't complicated, but it is certainly important. Be prepared to say what you do, for whom you do it, and what distinguishes you from other lawyers in your space. Talk about your experiences and the experience your client will have with you. This doesn't have to be difficult because it is simply expressing who you are as a businessperson. Practice, but don't let your anxiety rule the day.

CHAPTER 7

EVERY CLIENT IS A FRIEND
AND
EVERY FRIEND IS A CLIENT

A BUSINESS RELATIONSHIP is the same as any other relationship, except a business relationship is generally more one-sided than a traditional relationship. In a traditional relationship, both parties invest time, attention, and a genuine interest in getting to know the other. As they get to know each other, if they discover things they have in common, they naturally want to be around each other even more. Being kind, trusting, and polite is necessary; otherwise, the other party to the relationship will pull away. Being interesting and fun is important or the other party may get bored. Finally, there is what we call chemistry. The chemistry is created when all of these things come together.

A business relationship follows similar getting-to-know-you steps to those of a traditional relationship, and sometimes, when the chemistry is right with a potential client, you can develop a genuine friendship. However, most of the time your potential client may not be as interested in developing a relationship with you as you are in him or her. This does not mean that you should treat your potential client differently than any other new friend. On the contrary, to develop an above-average book of business, you must act as though it is a friendship, even if you are the only one participating.

What does this mean? It means you must invest time to develop the relationship. You have to pay attention to your potential client and let the individual know you are interested in him or her. People like attention, and if you are sincere, your potential client will appreciate the attention. Obviously, you cannot come on too strong or you will push your potential client away. Coming on too strong is annoying, so be careful not to be "that guy." The easiest way to avoid a negative response is to be sincere.

Being cheerful, kind, trusting, helpful, and polite should go without saying. Your potential client will not be a potential client for long if you do not focus on these basic rules of engaging other human beings. You learned these things in kindergarten. Remember them, practice them, and live them.

THE BOY SCOUT LAW
APPLIES TO YOUR BUSINESS

When I was a young teenager, I was active in the Boy Scouts. The Boy Scouts taught me about leadership and about how to be a good person. The Scout Law is instructive to all aspects of life. The Scout Law says:

A Scout is:

Trustworthy

Loyal

Helpful

Friendly

Courteous

Kind

Obedient

Cheerful

Thrifty

Brave

Clean

Reverent

Potential clients, like all people, prefer to build relationships with people who are interesting and fun. Some of us are naturally fun, and some of us find it easy to develop friendships; others not so much. If you feel that you are not one of the gifted ones who has an easy time with relationships, don't let that be an excuse. Don't allow that head trash to limit your success as a lawyer.

Personal and positive is more of a *perspective* than a personality. It can also be a priority, even if you are not naturally inclined to be that way. In my opinion, nearly anyone can be a good lawyer. Only those who commit to personal and positive relationships will build above-average books of business. The good news is that this simply takes commitment and attention to behaviors. It does not require that you restructure your personality.

For example, think about how you engage in conversation with others. The secret to becoming a good conversationalist involves two behaviors: 1) asking questions; and 2) listening more than you talk. There is no real magic to it—just a practiced attentiveness.

THE QUESTION: ONE OF YOUR BIGGEST ASSETS

I learned a long time ago that if one of my questions doesn't yield a useful or satisfactory answer, it's time to ask another question—one that's a bit deeper. If that question doesn't do the trick, it's time to ask another, until I get the information I need.

For example, I was trying to get to know a client who seemed a little on the nerdy side. When I asked the client, who had a background in economics, about his hobbies, he responded, "I don't have any hobbies. All I do is run my business."

I asked the next question, "What do you do on week-ends?"

He answered, "When I'm not working and not with my family, I watch Sunday morning television. I watch the world news."

Now I knew something important about my client. When I heard that Karl Rove and Howard Dean were coming to our city on a speaking tour, I knew I had something I could do with this client—something that would interest him. I purchased two tickets to the event and invited this client to attend. We had an amazing evening, attending the event and discussing politics over dinner. I don't see a reason to avoid a controversial top-ic—if the topic engages my client. I am simply careful to follow respectful, non-inflammatory guidelines.

As you learn the interests of your potential clients, be cu-rious. Choose to be (or if you must, act) interested in the things that interest your potential client. These behaviors will make you interesting to others. Droning on about your kids, your interests, or things that are important to you without checking the interest level of the other person will likely have the opposite effect. At best, the response will be neutral. You are much better off asking about the other person's kids, inter-ests, and things that are important to him or her.

How do you become fun? Is it even possible? Think about your experiences in high school, college, or your professional associations. Which people did everyone else want to be around? How did those individuals interact with others?

Again, I'm not suggesting you try to alter your personali-ty—just that you pay attention to others who are fun to be around. You can learn from people who have many friends. Such people smile and laugh. They are consistently cheerful.

They steer conversations toward the positive and upbeat and away from the negative. They don't do drama, and they are not complainers. They don't have fun at other people's expense. They have opinions without being offensive. They are willing to debate (or discuss) so as not to be a pushover, but they do so with courtesy and respect, and even a friendly manner. Others are attracted for all these reasons.

Pick someone as a role model, and examine that person's *behaviors*. Also, notice the pattern in your own life. Many adults grow up and leave their own versions of natural fun behind. You can be youthful without being childish, but many of us, consciously or unconsciously, believe we cannot. Recapture your own brand of fun.

Tim Sanders, author of *The Likeability Factor*, claims that likeable people outperform others and enjoy better health. He maintains you can raise your likability factor by improving the four elements of likability: friendliness, relevance, empathy, and realness. You don't have to be an extrovert or the life of the party to have these four characteristics. Being low-key and friendly is as appealing as being boisterous and friendly (sometimes more so).

You'll remember from an earlier chapter that people like to do business with people they *know, like, enjoy*, and *trust*. As you connect with the interests of your potential clients, they will be getting to know and like you. Because you are real and authentic, as well as competent, they will trust you. But how can you get them to *enjoy* you?

My strategy to building business relationships is to create a friendship, and it absolutely requires an above-average effort. If you want an above-average book of business, you have to put in above-average effort. You have to stand out.

Find out what your clients and referral sources do for fun and invite them to do it. You might have to get out of your comfort zone. I have played racquetball, gone shooting, played golf, ridden bikes, gone running, attended all sorts of professional sporting events, gone to dinner, gone to the theatre, and gone to art exhibits and museums with clients and referral sources. I have been on golf trips, big-game hunts, spa trips, and sailing trips.

Ask about your clients' kids and be interested in what those kids are into. Remember the kids' names and interests. Keep notes. If your potential clients have kids who are older than your kids are, ask for some advice. If your kids are older, then be doubly sure to focus the discussion on your potential clients' kids.

CURIOSITY NOT ONLY BUILDS RELATIONSHIPS, IT ENRICHES LIVES

Cultivating curiosity and openness to ideas that may not initially appeal to you can pay surprising dividends. Mark, a client, has an interest in mission work. For each of the last 20 years, Mark has taken a youth group to Appalachia for a week. As Mark spoke of this volunteer work to me at different times, I noticed his eyes light up with passion. So, although mission work was not something I had thought much about before, I asked questions, and I listened. I learned how terrific and rewarding it was for kids to fix houses, rebuild damaged structures, and clean up yards.

Because of Mark, I paid attention when a father of one of Danny's baseball teammates told me about an opportunity for Danny to go to the Dominican Republic on a baseball-themed mission trip. The father explained that for a week the boys would build a house in the morning and play baseball in the afternoon.

Naturally, I asked Mark what he thought of this opportunity. Mark's initial impression was akin to mine. The whole thing sounded a bit like an elitist opportunity, i.e., wealthy boys of one country paying to travel to play baseball with wealthy boys of another country. We imagined two sets of "haves" playing organized baseball on a manicured field. What's more, Mark reminded me, you don't have to go to the Dominican Republic to do mission work.

Even so, Mark and I decided I should ask more questions and dig a little deeper into this opportunity. When I got more information, I learned the trip to the Dominican was not about organized baseball at all. In fact, the Dominican kids Danny would meet would have no balls, no bats, no gloves—no shoes. The boys from the U.S. would be working to make overgrown fields playable and initiating pickup games with the Dominican boys. And they would be giving them gently used baseball equipment and shoes collected at home. In the morning, the boys would be building a house for a family living in a dilapidated shack. The family would be preselected by a mission group focused on helping poor Dominican families. Throughout it all, they would be developing a global perspective.

When I told Mark about what I learned, he was amazed and enthused. Danny has gone twice now, and as he puts it, "It changed my life."

Now Mark and I have a new point of connection, a deeper friendship. As a result of our connection, Mark has retained our Firm for some sophisticated corporate work and is helping me find a similar experience for our daughter Katie.

Showing interest in and involving a potential client's spouse or partner is a great way to get to know someone. It breaks down barriers that would otherwise exist in a business dinner. It makes it friendly. It makes it personal. Here's an example of how I once connected with something a potential client liked to do, involving our spouses. It involved a little creativity and worked out beautifully.

About 10 years ago, I wanted to get to know a potential client. He had told me that he and his wife loved to go to a particular restaurant near their house. He raved about how good the restaurant was, and I told him that my wife and I would try it someday.

On a late Friday afternoon, I emailed the potential client and told him that my wife and I were going to be "in their neighborhood" (we weren't) and were thinking about trying out their favorite restaurant. I invited him and his wife to join us. He replied that they would be there and would see us there. It looked impromptu, it was casual, it was convenient, and it worked. We had a lovely evening, and now he is one of my best friends.

When it comes to having things in common with a potential client, it is all about them. What they like to do, coincidentally, are the same things you like to do. If you think this is disingenuous, you are wrong. You are being a friend and building a relationship. It just happens that business is likely to follow.

As you can see, investing in a personal relationship with your clients and potential clients is not a nine to five endeavor. I spend approximately 1,000 hours a year on business development. I have coffee with a client, a potential client, or a referral source about three times per week. I do the same for lunch. Then, in the evenings, between kid activities, I do happy hour, networking events, and dinners at least twice a week. On weekends, I involve the kids or my wife. This might mean sharing a family activity like skiing, a ball game, hunting, or tennis. It might mean meeting at the park or the swimming pool. On weekends, my wife and I often go to dinner with a client, potential client, or referral source and his or her spouse. On occasion, we will go away for the weekend with another couple, and that couple will be close friends, but that other couple is usually connected to business in some manner.

Obviously, my professional life and personal life are intertwined in a manner that makes it impossible to tell what is personal and what is business. Therein is the secret code to a $1 million book of business. Remember the adage: Every friend is a client, and every client is a friend. There are no short cuts to this. If you are the type of person who thinks that it is important to separate business and friendships, then you will find it difficult to have a $1 million book of business. There is no trick to building personal relationships. You have to invest the time.

HOW ABOUT SOME SOCCER?

A lawyer I'd known for years moved to Southwestern Pennsylvania, where I live. Her husband, an extremely intelligent Texan and Naval Academy graduate, bought a business. With a few questions, I learned that he used to play soccer. I happen to play in an over-40 league, so it was easy to invite him to join. For two 10-week sessions in the winter indoor league and a 14-game spring and fall league, we play soccer and then gather for beer and wings afterward. His wife has said to me, "Thank God you are getting him out. Otherwise, he would do nothing!"

This man has become a good friend as well as a client. Recently, after a few drinks, he said that I was one of his best friends. That statement is particularly gratifying and a testament to my efforts in establishing *solid* relationships with my clients.

My time commitment and list of activities may over-whelm you. Perhaps you are shy, and extending yourself in these ways will be challenging. Perhaps you aren't physically active. If so, take baby steps. Be creative. Listen and learn what interests your clients and potential clients, and take some sort of action—making sure that action is more distinctive than sending an email!

For example, if a person mentions going to a vacation spot, send an article or guidebook via snail mail. When a person has a grandchild, send a gift. Invite a potential client to lunch, and include a guest who shares an interest, or a poten-tial referral partner. Invite a client to have breakfast at his or her favorite restaurant. Give the gift of tickets for the newest Pixar movie, Disney on Ice event, Globetrotters, professional sporting event, or the circus. The key is to do what interests the other person.

These actions are good starts, but remember this: There is no substitute for spending *actual time* with a client. A client can appreciate you, but not enjoy you, from a distance. You have to find a way to match your personality with the need to spend time with clients—at least if you want an above-average book of business.

I think that one of the keys to getting to know someone is being fun and making the things you do together fun. Many businesspeople are so caught up in their jobs or their compa-nies that they forget to have a hobby or engage in activities to have fun. Even your business meetings can include elements of humor and laughter. You can take the client's business seriously without taking yourself too seriously. As we said earlier, make business fun. When it stops being fun, it is time to do something else.

Finally, don't be afraid to expose yourself. No, not like that. Allow yourself to be vulnerable and real. Make it person-al by letting people see the softer side. When you do this, your clients, potential clients, friends, and referral sources feel special and connected—because you let them into the inner circle.

If you are not sure about how to do this, consider starting with what Simon Sinek calls "The Why." Talk about why you do what you do. Share your passion and talk about how the law excites you. Explain how you want to change the world, or at least contribute to it.

Also be willing to share your deeper, nonwork-related passions—at least the ones that are noncontroversial. Tap into your altruistic side, perhaps by adopting a charity, designating a volunteer day at your office, getting involved in something that has meaning in your life, hosting or sponsoring a fund-raiser. If you tap into a sincere altruistic passion and invest energy in that passion, you make the world a better place while connecting with others in meaningful ways.

As you open up about your passions, invite the other party to talk about his or hers. You just might find yourself on the path to a genuine friendship.

Make Sure to Be Personal, Positive, and Fun Inside the Office as Well as Outside

At our Firm, we get together once a month for happy hour. It is a scheduled time that everyone is encouraged to work into their calendars if they can. Sometimes happy hour is in the conference room. Sometimes we go to a local bar. In the summer, I grill hot dogs in the parking lot. The goal is to make working together fun by spending time together that does not involve work. We also have a firm-wide lunch once a quarter. We use this time to discuss high-level issues that affect the entire firm, but we also make it fun. There is always a video and something socially interesting on the agenda.

Recently, one of our lawyers asked to have a contest to encourage members of the Firm to live a healthier lifestyle. Every week a new challenge was issued, involving something to be accomplished every day that week. Items on the list included eating two servings of vegetables a day, exercising for 20 minutes, sleeping seven hours, writing down three things you are thankful for, and meditating for 10 minutes. These challenges provide a distraction to the workday and generate break-room conversation.

Our Firm also has a relay team for the local marathon. On occasion, we give prizes to lawyers who get their time in on time and support staff who have their filing done by week's end. In the spirit of March Madness, we have the traditional basketball pool and a ping-pong tournament. We have done doppelganger contests and baby picture contests.

Outside the office, when you are networking, approach it with the goal of meeting new friends. That makes it fun. Meeting new, interesting people *should* be fun. Rather than allowing yourself to be intimidated, think of networking as an adventure. Every networking event starts out like the first day of college. You have the ability to meet anyone you want, and the consequences are minor.

Don't forget to do what gets *you* jazzed. Make time for your family. Make time for your hobbies. In law school, my buddies and I used to say we needed to "sharpen our ax" when we felt like having some fun. This was our version of Stephen Covey's habit seven in the *7 Habits of Highly Effective People*: take time to sharpen your saw. Do something you really enjoy and refresh yourself. Sometimes you have to just get away and have what my wife calls "me time." We will cover this in more detail in Chapter 9. But it does not hurt if the thing you enjoy is something that involves other people. It doesn't matter whether you go to a bar, prayer group, concert, ball game, play, or evening class. If you choose an activity because it is fun, that activity can easily turn into an opportunity to meet someone interesting. Before you know it, that person may become your friend, your client, or both.

CHAPTER 8

CARE AND FEEDING OF YOUR CLIENTS

To be successful, every service professional has to expend energy in *getting* new clients. Profitability depends on *keeping* those clients. Thus, client satisfaction is our number one priority. The "proper care and feeding of clients" involves making them feel important and making them believe you are thinking about them. The following are important steps to create this reality. You'll recognize these steps from earlier chapters, but they are important enough to repeat.

GET TO KNOW YOUR CLIENTS

Develop your skills in asking questions and listening patiently to the answers. Get to know as much as you can about your potential clients. Where did they grow up? Where do they live now? Who are their spouses and kids? What do they do for fun? What are their biggest worries? What makes them most proud? What topics interest them?

SHARE VISION AND PASSION

A key element in building a lasting relationship with a client is connecting on their level of values. Ask your clients and potential clients about their values, and share your own. When you help your client to realize that your firm aligns with his or her values, you have a solid beginning for a mutually productive relationship. Post your values on your website and in your office. Refer to them frequently. Above all else, embody them.

GIVE YOUR CLIENTS REASON TO LIKE YOU

As you get to know your clients, they will get to know you. Let your guard down and let someone get to know you. Allow yourself to be personal. This is good practice, as long as you follow this basic rule: Listen more than you talk. Before you know it, you will be making a friend with someone who will lead you to business. Be a friend; have a friend.

If you are interested in your clients, they will like you and want to be around you more. They will also be more likely to give you business and refer you to others.

MAKE EXPERIENCES WITH YOUR CLIENTS ENJOYABLE

If you are interested in your clients as people, as well as open and transparent about yourself, clients will enjoy being around you.

This is especially true if you are positive and fun. When a client enjoys being around you, you have the beginning of a relationship. Make an investment in the relationship by doing things together outside of the office. This takes time, but the time is an investment in another human being and in the development of a client friendship.

GIVE YOUR CLIENTS REASON TO TRUST YOU

People are more likely to trust you if they know and enjoy you. Trust is the cornerstone in any relationship. Throughout every encounter, professionally and personally, behave in ways to earn the respect of your clients and potential clients. Be knowledgeable, respectful, professional, and ethical. As we have discussed, make commitments and keep them. This builds trust. Clients who trust you will tell you things you never imagined. Listen to them. Once you have established a reason for a client or potential client to know, like, enjoy, and trust you, you will have created a life-long relationship. These people will easily call on you for your advice and friendship. You will find that they will give you their business and referrals.

QUESTIONS TO START A CONVERSATION

Here are some of the questions I ask to initiate conversation, all of which may require appropriate follow-up:

1. Where do you live?

2. How long have you lived there?

3. Do you have a family?

4. How old are your kids?

5. What are they into?

6. Where did you grow up?

7. What do you do for a living? (How many employees? What is your geographical footprint? Do you have an exit strategy?)

8. How long have you been doing that?

9. What do you do for fun? And then finally, depending on how the conversation is going:

10. Do you want to get another drink?

11. I've really enjoyed talking with you. We should get coffee one of these days and get to know each other a little better.

12. It was nice talking with you. I am going to go say hi to some other people.

Manage Expectations with
Clear and Reasonable Response Times

As lawyers, one of the most important things we can do is communicate with our clients and manage their expectations. This isn't as hard as it may seem. Earlier in the book, I've referred to Justice James Brickley of the Michigan State Supreme Court, my first employer as a lawyer. Justice Brickley would often say, "If people would just say what they are going to do and then do what they say, the world would be a much better place." I've often thought about that and have quoted him in trying to get people to understand that managing expectations is not that difficult. We have to tell people what we are going to do, and then do it. Clients don't care as much about the timing as they do about knowing when to expect things to happen.

Don't allow yourself to feel pressured into promising to deliver a project quickly and then end up making a promise you can't fulfill. I once had a colleague who would tell a client that he would have the assignment completed in the next day or two, and then often miss the deadline.

Clients understandably get frustrated by missed deadlines and broken promises. I have had to do damage control on many occasions for this reason alone. We are better off providing a time frame that we are sure to meet. Typically, a client does not need you to complete a project immediately. In that case, give yourself a week, and then make sure you meet your stated deadline.

When there is an open-ended deadline, be sure to reach out regularly to tell your client where things stand. Experienced lawyers have a "spidey sense" that tells them that they have a client who is waiting to hear from them. When *you* get that feeling, reach out to your client immediately. Tell your client you are working on the project, and give yourself a deadline that you know you can meet.

When I get the feeling that a client needs to hear from me, I often use a simple strategy. I reach out to my client on a Thursday or Friday and inform the client that I am working on the project and will deliver it within a week—whether I have started on the project or not. That way I buy myself another week to complete the task, and I let my client know that I am thinking about him or her. This allows me to be a responsive provider while still balancing control of my schedule.

If your client calls or emails you to inquire about the status of a project, it is too late. You have already let the client down, and you will have used up a chip in the trust bank of the relationship.

Your goal should be to make a client feel as if he or she is your only client. However, on occasion, an emergency will come up for another client. In that case, contact your client and explain that an emergency has come up for another client that will cause you to miss a deadline. Clients understand that emergencies do come up. When it happens, I assure my clients that emergency delays are an exception to the way I practice. I assure them that if they ever have an emergency, I will drop what I am doing to make sure they are taken care of. I have never had pushback on that.

RETURN PHONE CALLS AND EMAILS WITHIN 24 HOURS

Strange as it may seem, the biggest complaint lawyers receive is that they don't return phone calls. As I've discussed several times already in this book, you should be thinking of that saying by Woody Allen, "Eighty percent of life is just showing up." What does it mean to show up in the practice of law? All we have to do is return our phone calls within 24 hours; tell a client what we're going to do; do what we say we will do; and treat people fairly and respectfully. With these simple actions, we are well beyond 80 percent of the way to success.

If you find yourself reluctant to return a client's call because you are neck deep in another project, make the call anyhow. There is nothing wrong with returning a call and telling a client that you don't have time to talk at that exact time because you are tied up with something else. Simply promise to call them at a future scheduled time. At the very least, have your assistant call the client to acknowledge the call and schedule a time for you to return the call.

A former colleague used to talk about "training" his potential clients and clients. He would say that you should not return your calls too quickly because you don't want your clients or potential clients to get used to that kind of treatment. This lawyer used to compare legal services with auto repair shops. When he calls for automobile service, he doesn't expect same-day or next-day treatment. What a lousy comparison.

Creating an expectation of delayed service or lack of concern for our clients' needs and schedules is far from the goal. This colleague's attitude toward training clients explains why he had a well-below-average book of business and why he is not a colleague anymore. We are in the service business, and clients require and expect service. If you do not return a client's call quickly, that person won't be a client for long.

With respect to potential clients who initiate a call, in my experience, whoever returns the call the quickest gets the business. I don't know how many times I have heard the words "Thank you for returning my call so quickly." When we return a call the same business day, we exceed the potential client's expectations.

Most of the time, potential clients who initiate a call have at least some experience working with a lawyer. Chances are a particular potential client will initiate a call because he or she has had a bad experience with a lawyer. Chances are even better that the bad experience included the lawyer not returning calls promptly. Now you have a potential client who is not expecting you to return his or her call the same business day.

When you do return the call that same day, you start the relationship by exceeding the potential client's expectations. Ninety-nine times out of 100, that person will become your client.

The same approach has to apply to emails. We live in an era where people are used to getting fast responses to any type of social or professional interaction. Our smart phones alert us to every single event that we allow them to, from a Facebook post, to the score of a game, to a court filing, to emails and texts. Because this is the case, don't fight it; embrace it. Return your emails as often as possible, but no less than once a day. Do you know anyone who doesn't respond to your texts or emails very promptly? Frustrating, right? Don't be that lawyer. Be that lawyer who is willing to communicate on a modern level. If you do, you will reap the benefits.

UNDER PROMISE AND OVER DELIVER

You have heard that we should under promise and over deliver. What does this mean in practice? It means that when we commit to a deadline, we make every effort to deliver the project *before* that deadline. It also means that if we estimate a particular amount of time or dollars for a project, our bill should be *less* than our estimate.

A former colleague who used to promise unrealistic deadlines also habitually told clients projects would cost half of what he knew they would end up costing. You can imagine how much this upset clients. Beware of this. I have had to do damage control many times to maintain relationships.

One of my first bosses at Reed Smith told me that when a client asks what a particular project will cost, we should estimate what we think it will take and then double it. I don't recommend going to such extremes that you will lose a project—only that you estimate in ways that allow you to surprise clients in good ways rather than bad ways when the bill comes due.

Admittedly, estimating cost is one of the hardest things we must do as lawyers. Face it head-on. Talk about it. Explain how hard it is. I tell clients that what we do is not science. It is not $2 + 2 = 4$. It is art. Contractors can calculate how many 2x4s it will take to build a house. Lawyers have to deal with opposing lawyers. When there is another human being on the other side, we have no way to predict whether that person will make the project easy or difficult. If that person is easy to deal with, the project will be less expensive. If that person is combative, the project will take more time and consequently cost more.

Other areas of over delivery include arriving early for meetings and greeting guests promptly when they come to see you. Clients expect to wait a reasonable amount of time; how great is it for them when you see them immediately. Again, you get to start an encounter by exceeding expectations.

Initiate Communication
and Head Off Breakdowns

While quick return phone calls and emails make a big positive impact, good communication, of course, is more complicated than that. Communicating effectively at work with our colleagues or clients, at home with our spouse or our kids, and even socially with our friends, is one of the biggest challenges we face. Most disputes, fights, arguments, divorces, and disagreements are the result of poor communication.

Good communication skills are essential to success in business and in life. As lawyers, we are supposed to be professional communicators, both in writing and verbally. Consequently, we must be ever vigilant to improving our communication skills and ensuring that we effectively communicate our thoughts to those we work with and work for.

Perhaps the biggest communication discipline surrounds listening. Good listening begins with giving 100 percent of your attention to what the other person is saying. It includes observing nonverbal cues, too. Good listening also involves asking clarifying questions; repeating back what you hear; sharing thoughts and reflections; and summarizing discussions. Good listening shows respect and leads to understanding, alignment, and rapport.

HOW TO MANAGE YOUR MEETINGS

I have taken numerous sales training classes, including Sandler Training. They taught me, among other things, the value of "actively" managing a meeting or conversation. I have learned that meetings are most effective when I patiently control the direction any meeting goes. Here are some steps to follow, in my words:

1. Address how much time is available to meet.

2. Talk about the agenda for the meeting.

3. State your ideal outcome from the meeting.

4. Discuss the reason you are together; that is, do your presentation, but don't give the answer away for free.

5. Always talk about the timing and cost of the service or project.

6. Offer to answer any questions and ask for a decision.

7. State that it is okay if the final decision is not to work together. A "no" is the next best answer to a "yes."

If you spend the majority of your time in any conversation listening, you are right where you should be. As a conversation moves to a close, however, good communication involves identifying action steps, including a clear understanding of who is responsible for each action and when that action needs to be completed. Communicating this information again in a follow-up email or document increases your communication effectiveness—and the likelihood that things will get done on time.

GIVE ADVICE

Twenty-plus years ago, when I started practicing law, it was common for a lawyer to say in response to a question about a business decision, "That is a business question, not a legal question. That is for the business guys to decide."

In the year I began my own firm, a client, the owner of a company, asked me about a business decision. I responded with the typical: "That is not a legal question; that is a business question." My client *firmly* told me that my response was rubbish. He said that I was smart and he thought I was a good businessman. He said he trusted my opinion and was willing to pay me for my opinion. He said, "I don't give a f*** whether my question is a business question or a legal question. If you don't want to give me your opinion, I need another lawyer. I want to know what you think."

Beginning with that encounter, I stopped shying away from giving clients business advice. Many of my clients are CEOs of privately owned companies who often need guidance in many different areas of business. Sometimes a client needs to be given options and a solid recommendation. Sometimes a client is simply too close to a situation to see it objectively. Perhaps the client has never had to deal with that particular issue before. As a lawyer representing many companies, chances are I've had to deal with that issue in the past. Even if I have not, my legal mind and general business experience puts me in a unique position to give advice on the topic. Similar things are true for you as well, no matter what your area of legal practice.

Except from an absolute purist point of view, lawyers are, in a sense, consultants. Clients pay us for our advice, and we should be willing to give it to them. Being a trusted advisor to your clients makes you invaluable to them.

Don't be afraid to disagree with a challenging client. This is part of the communication process. Listen actively, respond honestly, keep it rational, but don't forget to sprinkle in some passion when necessary—I call it professional indignance. Agree to disagree if acceptable, but always maintain respect, even when disagreeing. This will pay off in the long run. You will find that you will have a longtime client and friend.

At the risk of stating the obvious, your advice has to be solid. Explain there are no guarantees. Explain the pros and cons to a particular decision, and explain the risks. If you do this with conviction, saying, "If it were me, here is what I would do," you will have a longtime client. Once you enter into the circle of trust, you will find your clients coming back to you for more and more advice.

CREATE AN EXPERIENCE FOR CLIENTS

In his popular TED Talk, Simon Sinek explains how our society has transformed its buying habits over the years. According to Sinek, we started as a consumer society, in which we bought stuff simply because it met a practical need or otherwise appealed to us. From there, we moved to a service-oriented society, in which we expected more than basic stuff from our suppliers. In other words, we looked for "added value." Today, consumers seek even more than added value; we seek *experience*. Sinek uses Starbucks and Lexus as examples to demonstrate how people buy an experience.

I believe Simon Sinek is correct in his analysis of consumer behavior, and I embrace it. When we provide an experience for our clients, we distinguish ourselves from our competition. Those who want to have an above-average book of business have to think beyond selling a product such as a brief or a will. We have to think beyond selling a service such as assisting a business in a loan transaction. We have to think about the experience that our clients have when they come to us for advice.

Starbucks is all about a cool space with comfortable chairs and plenty of tables and outlets, where you can hang out and work or study for as long as you want and maybe buy coffee. What's the parallel for a team of legal professionals? How can we provide an experience for our clients?

I stand by what I said in Chapter 1: Above all, lawyering is a relationship business. A good lawyer knows the law, and applies that law as an art *on behalf of people*. We provide an experience for clients by making all of our practices and encounters *personal*. This is why in nearly every chapter I have emphasized the need to invest a great deal of time, energy, and money in face-to-face interactions with clients, potential clients and referral sources.

When you make those interactions sincere, creative, and fun, you create an experience. When you treat every client as a friend who deserves a timely response and a personal interest, you create an experience that keeps clients and referrals coming back. You cannot accomplish this goal with tricks or techniques like an email or newsletter campaign. You build a $1 million book of business with face-to-face encounters.

It's not uncommon for me to get a compliment that goes like this, "I've never met a lawyer like you." That's when I know I'm doing things right. You can generate this same response—and watch your business grow in the process.

CHAPTER 9

CARE AND FEEDING OF YOURSELF

THE OLD SEXIST SAYING, "A happy wife is a happy life," rings true when we update it to say, "A person who has healthy relationships outside of work is happier and more attractive to others than a person who does not." Two examples point to this truth.

I worked with a single female lawyer who lacked significant relationships, either with an intimate partner or with friends. While I don't know the dynamic behind this, I do know that the woman was lonely, perhaps depressed, and miserable. I saw it reflected in every interaction with colleagues and even clients. No one was eager to be around her.

The same was true of a male colleague who was embroiled in a bitter divorce. During the two and a half years of his extended battle, this man was miserable—and it showed in every one of his interactions too, with the same impact on others. People are not attracted to service professionals who pull them down emotionally, no matter how great that service professional's skills.

When I talk about caring for yourself, I'm talking about it in the context of business. Our profession is demanding, and as a lawyer, you need to do things you wouldn't choose on a regular basis. Certain habits will make you better at managing these demands over the long haul.

I have noticed that service professionals who have balance in their lives are more grounded than others. Balance leads to a variety of interests—which makes a person interesting to others. Balance leads to a more satisfied, positive, and meaningful life, which makes a person more attractive as a person and as a service provider.

I'm not suggesting that it's *always* possible to maintain healthy and fulfilling relationships. Intimate and family relationships get complicated. I am suggesting that you recognize that all your important relationships affect your state of mind and the way you interact with others. It's in your best business interest to give those relationships the attention and care they require.

Research shows that people seek business connections, as well as personal ones, with people who are similar to them. This may not be fair, but it does you no good to fight it. If people cannot find a connection with you, they probably won't want to do business with you.

Do everything you can to fit into natural situations where you can connect with potential and active clients. Find ways to interact in the community you wish to serve. If you believe you are mainstream, then swim in the main stream. If you are not, then swim in the stream where others are like you. For example, if you are a divorce lawyer, coach a kids' soccer team. If you are an estate lawyer, get on the board of the local community center. If you are a business lawyer, volunteer for a leadership position in a business organization in your community. What is important about this is that you are sincere and do what is important to you. Do and/or be involved in things you are passionate about. You will find that these efforts will lead to business opportunities.

I rely upon my wife, Susan, to support my business development efforts. Susan accepts my need to do the networking activities that allow me to meet new people continually. She also accepts and supports my "every friend is a client and every client is a friend" approach. That means Susan is willing to talk about what I do as well as share dinner, social events, parties, and other activities with clients. She welcomes my clients into our personal life and our family activities. Together we make it fun for everyone involved, including our kids.

BUSINESS RELATIONSHIPS AND FAMILY RELATIONSHIPS ARE PARALLEL PRIORITIES

I don't take Susan's support of my business for granted. In fact, I intentionally and consistently invest in our marriage. I believe that everything I've said about investing in clients applies to our significant others as well.

Don't think for an instant that integrating my family priorities and business priorities was easy. It wasn't always as it is now. At first, Susan resisted and was disinterested. At times, she was blatantly unsupportive. However, after a while, after Susan observed what her participation meant for my practice, what it meant for us to maximize earning potential, she began to understand the importance of the principles outlined in this book and got on board. Though it might not be apparent to the casual observer, she has been an instrumental contributor to the Firm's success.

This dynamic is not a one-way street. I have made an investment in my wife's life and paid attention to her priorities and passions. I'm committed to date nights, and I bring flowers home for no reason. I try to be interesting when I am with Susan, and I try to be likeable. I even watch the Food Channel's show *Chopped* because Susan likes it, and I have occasionally taken our kids to watch her tennis matches.

I understand that Susan adapts and sacrifices for my needs —a lot—and I work to make it a reciprocal relationship. I make time to do with her those things she enjoys, and I don't ever, ever act as though it is a chore or an accommodation. To the contrary, I have found that by following the principle of making experiences fun and positive, I have enjoyed these things. Not surprisingly, I have even managed to get several clients from encounters that support my investment in Susan.

Susan and I are raising four children, and we seek to be engaged parents. I have an interpersonal relationship with each of our children. I'm concerned about their interests and their needs. I spend focused time with each child. Because of the disproportionate amount of time that I spend with Danny with sports and other "guy" activities as compared to our three girls, and because of the dilution that exists for a parent with four kids, I spend one weekend a year away from home with each daughter, one on one, at a destination of her choosing. We call these weekends Daddy and Daughter Weekends. We have been all over the Eastern United States, and each daughter has come to look forward to these weekends. I have come to cherish them as well. The time I have spent with our daughters, one on one, has created some of my best memories. I love going into their rooms and looking at the collages of pictures of the various weekends we have spent together and talking with the girls about those memories.

I find that raising our children has parallels to managing employees—in that I need to know, respect, and motivate the individuals involved. In each case, a sincere investment is needed. I don't get to be too busy for my wife or my kids. I don't get to presume that my own agenda is more important than theirs.

Keeping Yourself Energized and Refreshed Makes Good Business Sense

Building and growing a business is a demanding occupation. Investing in healthy relationships is demanding as well. I'm committed to making every day and task as fun as possible, but I'm not always enjoying myself or feeling confident. Just like you, I am often doing something I'd prefer not to do. Not everything we do can be wonderful all of the time. However, I am pretending to enjoy it, and that makes all the difference.

You cannot keep up the pace of maintaining an above-average book of business and healthy relationships unless you build in some time for yourself. "Me" time is different for everyone, and only you can figure out what works for you. Once you figure out how you like to spend your "me" time, build it into your schedule and leave the guilt behind. Consider your "me" time as an investment in yourself, which is essential to meeting your family and business goals. When you cheat yourself out of reenergizing, you cheat the others and the business that depends upon you. You can pretend this isn't true for a while, but the neglect will catch up with you. If you struggle with guilt, remind yourself that taking care of yourself will make you better at developing business. It will also make you a better spouse and parent. It is like putting the oxygen mask on yourself in an airplane emergency before helping others.

In order to keep myself refreshed, I've run four marathons and participated in one Olympic-distance triathlon and numerous sprint triathlons. I've climbed Mt. Shasta, to the top of Pikes Peak, and to Phantom Ranch at the bottom of the Grand Canyon. I have hiked in over 25 national parks and have gone on several high-adventure hunting trips and fishing trips. I attend three annual golf weekends. I play indoor soccer in an over-30 league and outdoor soccer in an over-40 league. By temperament, I'm aggressive, and training for soccer, a race, or a high-adventure trip feeds into my natural drive. Being in shape for these events requires me to train regularly, and the training allows me to feel refreshed. Every time I train, I clear my head and care for my body. What's more, I can talk about these events and use them as a way to meet people. Sometimes, I train with a group comprised of all different types of professionals, which has the added value of connecting me with potential clients and referral sources.

Running marathons and high adventure may not be for you, but some activity, any activity, will work equally well. When you find that activity, embrace it, love it, and use it as an escape and as a way to engage with others. Don't be surprised when you get a client or two from your activities. And it's a great way to keep your ax sharp. Remember the concepts discussed in Chapter 7.

THINK OF THE CHALLENGES OF BUSINESS AS A GAME

Building a business is work, but you can think of it as a game. This different perspective can energize you.

Thinking of business as a game allows you to experiment and learn along the way. For example, if you try a new elevator pitch at a networking event and it bombs, don't think of it as a failure. Think of it as a learning experience and move on. It's sport. If you don't experiment, you won't give yourself the opportunity to grow.

Don't allow yourself to indulge in an attitude that fearfully says, "If I don't get a client this week, I won't eat." If you indulge in this kind of head trash, it will reflect in your interactions. People can sense fear and/or a lack of confidence. This is a death nail. Discipline yourself to think and act positively, and you'll attract others.

Do you remember the restaurant scene from *When Harry Met Sally*? Meg Ryan, as Sally, does her elaborate imitation of a faked orgasm. Afterward, the server asks another patron for her order. The woman, nodding toward Sally, says, "I want what she's having."

When you discipline yourself to dwell on the positive, you might even glow like Sally—even if you have to fake it. The point is, you won't have to fake it for long. If you make being positive and cheerful a way of life, soon you will find that it comes naturally. And it builds on itself. The more positive and cheerful you are, the more people will want to be around you and the more success you will have, which will make you more positive and cheerful. Soon you will be glowing more than your competitor who is always complaining.

In addition to cultivating positive thoughts, cultivate a curious attitude. Get out of your routine; stretch yourself. As we discussed earlier, be interested and interesting. Ask questions. Go places. Engage in new experiences. Even become more interesting to *yourself*. Sometimes you won't like what you try, but the experience will give you something to talk about. Often, a new experience requires that you concentrate—and get out of your daily stress mode. Often, adventures allow you to meet new people naturally and might even connect you to a potential client or referral source. Even if you don't get this type of direct result, a variety of experiences will make you a well-rounded person, and this reflects in the way you interact with others.

YOUR THOUGHTS AND HABITS
DRIVE EITHER SUCCESS OR FAILURE

Viewing business as a game is a *mental perspective* that can become a productive habit. It changes the drudgery that says, "I *have* to do this" to "I *get* to do this and see what happens."

While the old advice to think of your glass as half full rather than half empty may seem overused and trite, the advice points to a fundamental truth. If you wake up every day and say, "The weather in this town sucks," you are sure to have a gloomy day. You will be bringing the negative energy into the day yourself. Naturally, your energy will be low, and your resistance to success will be high. If you approach enough days like this, the perspective will become a habit, and you'll consistently hover in the zone of discontent. It will reflect in everything you do. And, believe me, people notice.

If you think I'm being unrealistic, remember the story I told in Chapter 1 about cleaning latrines with a group of Boy Scouts? Obviously, none of us wanted to clean latrines, but when we set goals for ourselves, we completed the job in record time, had fun, and built comradery in the process. You can do this within your own mind as well as with your colleagues. Almost everything in life can be fun—if you *decide* to see it that way. Remember Donna from Chapter 2—the woman behind the cash register? "People need to lighten up. It's like … man, we're alive."

You can rise above old habits of negativity and low energy. For example, I've learned that training for and running a marathon is a mental game. To successfully train and get to the finish line, I have to control my mind and avoid talking myself into quitting, which is quite easy come mile 20. Building a business is a mental game as well. I have learned to control negative thoughts, not panic when things are slow or something goes badly, and make it fun, when it could easily not be.

Standing before a judge is a mental game, too. No matter how nervous you feel, you can still tell yourself, "I know this material better than anyone. I can do this. I can act confident and in control."

It can be particularly hard to control our minds when we make a mistake, lose a case, or lose a friend. We tend to set superhuman expectations and then malign ourselves when we don't achieve those expectations. When a case goes to trial, the nature of litigation means that 50 percent of us lose every time. When we are the loser, we can berate ourselves, or we can appreciate what we learned from the experience.

There is no reason to allow losses to define us. Find value in yourself, not in your deals, your wins, or your losses. Taking losses personally is easy; we must resist the urge to allow that. We are natural competitors and want to win. And that desire to win, by its nature, lends itself to allowing ourselves to make our clients' problems our own problems. If you do this, you won't be in practice long, and if you are, you won't be happy about it.

A legend in baseball coaching, Tommy Lasorda, once said, "No matter how good you are, you're going to lose one-third of your games. No matter how bad you are, you're going to win one-third of your games. It's the other third that makes the difference." Don't let losing define you!

As a professional service provider, think of yourself as similar to a professional athlete. Every professional athlete makes bad plays, sometimes with championships and huge amounts of money at stake. The pressure to perform well is enormous.

Great athletes respond to each bad play by forgetting about it and focusing on the next play. Mike Krzyzewski, the head coach of Duke University's men's basketball team, has won more games than any other men's college basketball coach. He is renowned for his leadership skills and is famous for saying "next play" after every single play in all of his games. This is his way of telling his team to forget what just happened, whether it was good or bad, and to focus on what is coming next. His mantra: Next play.

> ### THIS IS HOW COACH KRZYZEWSKI
> ### DESCRIBES HIS PHILOSOPHY
>
> In basketball and in life, I have always maintained the philosophy of "next play." Essentially, what it means is that what you have just done is not nearly as important as what you are doing right now. The "next play" philosophy emphasizes the fact that the most important play of the game or life moment on which you should always focus is the next one. It is not about the turnover I committed last time down the court, it's not even about the three-pointer I hit to tie the game, it is about what's next.
>
> To waste time lamenting a mistake or celebrating success is distracting and can leave you and your team unprepared for what you are about to face. It robs you of

> the ability to do your best at that moment and to give your full concentration. It's why I love basketball. Plays happen with rapidity and there may be no stop-action. Basketball is a game that favors the quick thinker and the person who can go on to the next play the fastest.

In the practice of law, it's always time to move to the next play, the next event, the next case, the next client, the next first-time appointment. True professionals don't indulge in hanging their heads and berating themselves. They learn from the mistake, refocus, and move forward. This is how you care for yourself in the midst of a high-stakes mental game.

I've made a lifetime habit of controlling my thoughts and maintaining a positive frame of mind. I never expected to be tested as sorely as I was in August of 2014, when the afore-mentioned group of colleagues betrayed me by plotting behind my back, leaving without notice—and taking some of my own clients and support staff members with them.

As you know from Chapter 1, this was one of the most horrible experiences of my life. At first, I had self-doubts, low energy, and questions about the confidence I'd always found easy to have. My positive attitude was on its thinnest ice. I examined myself, consulted with trusted advisors and peers, and took a hard look at how I ran my business and who I was as a person and a leader. I learned some things and made some changes.

One of the hardest parts of this experience was examining my frame of mind. I had invested myself in a group of people who demonstrated a clear lack of character, took all I could give them, and then betrayed me. They didn't just leave the Firm; they attacked my livelihood. Would this experience change me, leaving me bitter, untrusting, and negative? I reminded myself what I frequently tell my kids and what I have mentioned a couple of times already in this book: The true character of a person is tested when his or her chips are down.

I decided that, in fact, I would not let the experience change or define me. While I accept that some people will behave in an unprofessional and unscrupulous manner, living in that state of fear, paranoia, and negative dimension puts you in their world. When you live in a sewer, is a rat the thing to be? I say no. I choose to believe that most people are trustworthy, and that it is good business and life affirming to build positive, productive, and even fun relationships with clients and colleagues. In the long run, you will be farther ahead, not only monetarily, but in self-worth, respect from others, peace of mind, happiness, and legacy.

As 2015 ended, 15 months after the betrayal, our Firm was back up to 11 lawyers, and revenue was higher than ever. Moreover, the employees of The Lynch Law Group voted the Firm one of the top 100 best places to work in *The Pittsburgh Business Times'* annual survey. At the end of 2016, we were up to 14 lawyers, had just completed our best year ever in terms of revenue, and again were voted by the employees as one of the top 100 best places to work in the Pittsburgh region. Most recently, 2017 ended with 17 lawyers and was our best year to date.

I contend that the habits of thought and behavior I had fostered over my 40+ years prior to this incident gave me what I needed to weather it. Good habits can develop character muscles that give you strength when you need it. I can say working through this experience has ultimately made me a better—and even happier—person. I'm a better employer, spouse, father, and friend.

CHAPTER 10

COMMIT TO COURAGE

OVER 16 YEARS AGO, I stumbled upon a lesson in perception that has guided me ever since. At the time, I was a senior associate at Reed Smith, working long hours and feeling as if something was missing. That something was the involvement in a business of some sort. In college, I had started a swimming pool cleaning and service company—Sun Lover Pools. That business allowed me to pay my own way through college and law school. When one of the partners at Reed Smith referred to my void as an entrepreneurial itch that I needed to scratch, I realized he was right. So I did.

My friend Jack and I bought five cottages on two acres at the foothills of the Laurel Mountains just east of Pittsburgh, Pennsylvania, in a quaint little town called Ligonier. The area, known as Laurel Highlands, is a beautiful four-season destination. It features spectacular natural scenery, outstanding outdoor recreation venues, historic sites, and plenty of family activities.

The cottages were originally built as summer places, just after World War II. Jack and I refurbished the cottages, made them all-season, built a website, and got ready to reopen the business. We set the rent below market, at $50 per weeknight, and $75 per weekend night, in attempt to gain market share.

Nobody called. We had no web activity. It was a bust.

I wondered if, by pricing below market rate, we were sending the message that the place was a dump. To test our hypothesis, we raised the rate to $100 per weeknight and $125 per weekend night, and $190 for both Friday and Saturday nights.

The phone started ringing, and I learned something I will never forget: perception *is* reality. This is true on multiple levels. The clothes you wear, the car you drive, the office space you choose, the way you shake hands, and the amount of money you charge all contribute to the perception people have of you. The sweet spot, where you attract the best-fit client, isn't always easy to find. If you want to have an above-average book of business, you have to search for that spot. Finding and sticking to that sweet spot takes some determination—and courage.

When I started The Lynch Law Group in 2002, I set my rate at $150 per hour, well below the market I was in and thinking that a low rate would help me get busy quicker. Not much business came in. Remembering my lesson from the cottages, I raised my rate to $225 per hour—and the business began to come in. Given that my firm is a business boutique, I had to be careful not to set my fees at a price point of the larger firms in town, but not so low that I would be perceived as low quality.

FIND AND EMBRACE YOUR SWEET SPOT

We have an unconscious cultural perception that says, "If you are expensive, you must be good. If you are cheap, I am not sure you know what you are doing." I can't explain this human phenomenon, but I know it's there.

Once you find your sweet spot and get busy, you have a choice to make. You can rejoice and work like crazy—or you can raise your rates again. I suggest the second choice, where you can work less and make the same or more money. You are likely to lose some clients and gain different ones that are more desirable. Who doesn't want to work less and earn more?

It takes courage and some experimenting to push the limits of your sweet spot, and it is complicated by the fact that your sweet spot moves with the economy and supply and demand. When the economy is healthy, I raise my rates at the beginning of each year. I practice quoting the new rate to potential clients. If 50 percent of the potential clients wince, I know I've gone too high. If only 20 percent wince, I know I'm in a good spot. If my wince-ratio is too high, I can lower the rate with the next potential client.

If you are balking at this practice, it may be that you don't believe you deserve higher rates, for any number of reasons. Here is the truth: If you have the skill and can provide the service to exceed customer expectations, you deserve the fee. Any other concept is head trash.

You might also fear that you'll lose potential clients (and needed income) if you quote the higher rate. You might. You will definitely lose clients if you don't believe you deserve the fees you quote, which in turn will make you lose confidence, which in turn will make you lose clients. It can turn into a nasty downward cycle.

Don't be afraid of damaging your reputation. There are many clients out there. If you are polite and professional, the worst someone will say about you is that you are expensive. That's not necessarily a bad thing.

Most people find talking about money uncomfortable. But, you have to talk about the money. To avoid the awkwardness of talking about money, train yourself to quote your rate with confidence. At The Lynch Law Group, we practice quoting our fees. I tell my colleagues to look in the mirror and say, "My hourly rate is . . ." Watch your facial expressions as you do this; notice your body language; and practice until you can quote your rate with confidence. Remind yourself that you are worth it. If you don't quite believe it, keep practicing, and fake it until you believe it. You *are* worth it.

If the reason you struggle believing you deserve the rates you charge is that you recently graduated, or even if you are a seasoned lawyer who has trouble with this, I want you to think of this as stepping up to your profession. In our culture, lawyers are one of a number of time-honored, well-respected professions. Doctors, lawyers, and engineers all complete rigorous academic and, in some cases, practical studies before they meet the qualifications of their profession. Accordingly, we attribute respect to people who are members of these professions. We put them on pedestals. You are now a member of that club. As you think about your rate, put yourself in a potential client's shoes. From this person's perspective, you have the credentials. Allow yourself to be on the pedestal. Embrace it. You've earned it. The fact that people put you on a pedestal is an advantage. Use it.

I'm not suggesting you behave like a jerk—only that you wear your credentials with confidence and ask for the fee you have earned. In the popular sitcom *M*A*S*H*, both Hawkeye and Dr. Charles Winchester III were fully competent physicians. Hawkeye carried his credentials and expertise with grace and humor. Winchester carried his with insolence. People flocked to Hawkeye and avoided Winchester.

It takes courage to look someone in the eye and quote a fee, especially if you are young and/or need the business. You fear rejection or even ridicule. You'll remember from Chapter 5 that researcher Brené Brown has found that we universally feel vulnerable when the possibility of rejection exists. In discussing fees, this possibility is real, and the stakes are high.

The stakes are high for the other parties in these transactions too. Most of our potential clients find the conversation about money uncomfortable as well. If you feel uncomfortable talking about money, say so. Brené Brown tells us that it takes courage to admit the discomfort that you feel. If you do admit the discomfort, however, you open the door for a greater connection and conversation. You don't have to sound pathetic or wishy-washy to initiate a money conversation with these words: "I'm uncomfortable bringing up money, but we obviously need to discuss it." Your authenticity can be disarming in a situation in which a potential client fears being in a competitive and perhaps intimidating position. Your authenticity allows the two of you to perceive your work together as a win-win. I'm not suggesting that you reduce your fee in the discussion that follows, simply that you be authentic about the discomfort you feel discussing it.

PRACTICE HOW YOU WANT TO PLAY—REPRISE

In Chapter 3, I described how I talk to our son, Danny, about practicing how he wants to play baseball. Being around Danny and his friends as they've developed their baseball skills over the years, I've seen a lot of hotshot-kid behavior. Of course, I had my own boyhood days of hotshot behavior too—but I continually tell Danny that such behavior on the practice field is self-sabotage. I tell Danny to *practice how you want to play.*

Here's what I mean: If a batter who takes 10,000 practice swings goofs off for half of those swings, that batter has only practiced 5,000 swings. He or she has wasted the other 5,000. Serious ball players look at every ball, at the plate or in the field, as if it is the 9th inning, and the game is on the line. The more a player practices this way, the easier and more natural it will be to face that scenario in real life. This is how Olympic athletes practice. Practicing how you want to play creates muscle memory, amazing levels of single-point focus, and confidence.

In legal situations, successful lawyers must exhibit a persona of confidence. To make this easy and natural, practice when you aren't in legal situations. You can conduct yourself with confidence anytime you do anything, even if you don't feel confident.

For example, how do you project confidence if you happen to be a spectator at your child's athletic event? You don't necessarily need to wear a coat and tie, but you should groom and dress well. You don't necessarily need to have the most expensive car in the lot, but you shouldn't have a junker either. Cheer appropriately, and even enthusiastically, for the kids—all the kids.

There's a paradox here. Projecting confidence doesn't involve being uppity or superior. It is sending forth a sense of comfort in your own skin, no matter the social or professional situation. The paradox is that even while exhibiting such confidence, you may be terrified inside. However, only in the silence of your heart or in the presence of your most trusted advisor, friend, spouse, or therapist should you reveal your insecurities.

DON'T BE AFRAID TO BE GREAT

Many people, perhaps most people, are held back by fear. Fear of losing? Maybe it is the fear of winning? What does that mean? Winning adds complexity and responsibility to your life. When you are on top, there is only one direction to go—down! That is scary and can be painful. When you win, people look at you differently. You might be expected to lead, the way the best player on the team becomes the team captain. You might find that uncomfortable.

President John F. Kennedy once quoted Luke 12:48 in a speech: "To whom much is given, much is expected." I believe this and live by it. It is easy to be average. For some people, losing may even provide a safe zone, a secret relief held only in the silence of their hearts. If you don't try, if you don't put yourself out there, you don't have to ever face rejection. You don't have to ever deal with the risk of failure. For most people, it is more comfortable to not try than to deal with the demons of rejection and failure.

Perhaps even more than the result, the effort that must go into achieving the result is what matters. It is hard to work hard. It is hard to consistently do the behaviors that it takes to be great. If it were easy, everyone would do it. Either way, if you want to be great, if you want to build a $1 million book of business, you will have to overcome the head trash associated with rejection and the apathy that most people have toward hard work. I tell our kids every morning when I drop them off at school: "Don't be afraid to be great. Do something great today."

Consistently practice how you want to play, and it will become your reality—because perception is reality. You'll believe this reality, and others will believe it too. You will exude confidence, build success, and you won't need to practice saying your rate in the mirror anymore.

CHAPTER 11

BUILDING A LARGE PRACTICE

HOW DO YOU KNOW when to take the leap from a sole practitioner, a partner, or an aspiring partner at a firm to the head of your own law practice? If you've been practicing the behaviors described in this book, at some point you will reach a critical mass. You will reach a number of clients and billable hours that you can no longer service on your own. You will reach a point at which meeting your promises to clients will become increasingly more difficult, and it will mean that you have no time to be out of the office generating new relationships. When that happens, it will be time to make a choice.

CHOOSE YOUR OWN PATH

Initially, I had no thought of leaving Reed Smith where I worked for six years. I had a lucrative career and was one year away from making partner when I was presented with an opportunity to run a start-up company. I was intrigued. The dot-com bubble was at its peak. "Going Public" was very popular. Getting stock options was a standard condition of employment. I looked around the "room" at Reed Smith and reflected.

> Our first child was only two years old. I wondered what I would be able to say to him when he asked for my advice about a possible job opportunity when he was 25 or 30 years old. I contemplated how shallow it would be for me to say: "I don't know. I've never worked anywhere other than Reed Smith for the last 30 years." What would be my perspective? How could I advise him, or any of our future children, when my only job was in the ivory tower of a white bread law firm?
>
> I wanted something more. I wanted experience and adventure. I was not ready to become middle aged at 30 years old.

The choice before you is straightforward: Option 1 is to stop growing. Option 2 is to hire someone to help you do the work.

Like every person who both *sells* a product or service (widgets or lawyering) and *produces* that product or service (widgets or lawyering), you live with a tension. Your success depends upon you constantly generating new business while doing an excellent job in delivering on your promises to current clients. A breakdown on either end of this equation spells stress, disappointment, and sometimes, disaster.

There is no shame in choosing to stop growing. There are plenty of reasons to make that choice. If you want to grow an above-average book of business, however, you will have to choose to leverage other people's time to free yourself up to get out of the office and get more work. You must learn to delegate.

If you decide that you do not want to delegate, two things will be true. First, you will have created a job for yourself. You will have not built a business. Owning a business means you employ people, beyond an administrative assistant. Second, there is risk, a certain fear, that some of your existing clients will go away—for whatever reason. If that happens, and chances are it probably will, you will have been too busy serving clients to have the network that would otherwise continue to feed your pipeline.

If you choose to delegate and manage the process well, you will hit another critical mass of clients and billable hours, requiring you to hire yet again. You are on your way to building a business.

DEVELOP A HIRING STRATEGY

It makes sense to start by hiring someone to perform the less sophisticated work. You might think of it as someone to perform the basics—the "young associate" work. This is a good start to growth, but it isn't the only workable strategy. And it is not a strategy that lends itself to a $1 million book of business.

As an individual lawyer, you can't be deeply immersed in every area of law that your clients might need. If you choose to hire another lawyer who has a different but related subject matter focus, you expand the capabilities of your practice. For example, as a business law firm, I have clients who need expertise on employment law, real estate, and mergers and acquisitions, among other areas. A practice focused on family law may need expertise in child custody, adoption, and divorce.

By hiring lawyers who focus in diverse but related areas, you can round out a suite of services and offer comprehensive counsel to clients.

There may be times, of course, when you don't need or aren't quite ready for another full-time lawyer. You can seek out a lawyer who has some clients of his or her own but who still needs work. Ideally, you will bring this person into your firm and pay him or her a wholesale hourly rate. At worst, that person stays independent, but you still do well to try to negotiate a wholesale rate. A similar relationship can exist with a "contract" lawyer. Services and websites are available to match up contract lawyers with law firms that have overflow work. This is a low-risk way to find someone you can work with, but it is usually temporary. Those contract lawyers are contract lawyers for a reason. When you find someone you like, try to hire that person outright before someone else does. Plus, a contract lawyer is not "all-in" at your firm. You want someone who is 100 percent committed to your practice and your clients.

Another option is to seek out a sophisticated lawyer who no longer wants to work full time. That lawyer may come via two different ways. First, a senior lawyer might want to reduce hours for any number of good reasons. For example, as life spans keep increasing and people worry about their savings lasting 30 or more years, many knowledgeable and skilled professionals are seeking to work part time to stretch out their dollars. Second, there are excellent lawyers out there who, due to family circumstances or other reasons, don't want to work full time but still want to be involved in practicing law.

This may be a highly qualified stay-at-home mom who worked at a large firm in the beginning of her career and is ready to go back to work—only part time, or perhaps full time but with a different work-life balance than she had at the large firm. Chances are, she won't be building a book of business, and if she tells you she wants to build a book of business, great, but you need to address her sincerity. You can't build a practice working at it part time. Accept that and acknowledge it. Once you do, you will have a great resource and someone who can provide excellent work for your clients. Or even better, you will have that *and* someone who will bring revenue into the firm.

If you choose this option, I recommend you hire the person as an employee, not a contract lawyer. Give the person office space and treat him or her as part of your practice. Make the lawyer part of the team. The goal is to have the person both physically and emotionally present in your firm.

When you hire someone to work part time, the financial arrangement can be tricky. You may pay by the hour or estimate the workload and provide a commensurate salary. If you pay by the hour, you will have to provide a higher hourly rate, given that the employee is bearing all the risk of a slow period. If you guarantee a salary, you can offer a lower amount, given that you are bearing all the risk of there being work available.

INTERVIEW CAREFULLY

When I first started my practice, I used to say, "Give me the smartest, hardest working person I can find, and I will teach them the rest." That was a mistake. Over time, I realized that the bedrock principles that underlie my approach to life and my practice (detailed in Chapter 2) are more difficult to find. Plus, teaching someone to do the work right and to keep their promises is harder than it sounds, if not impossible. Either you are that kind of person, or you aren't.

Now, when I am hiring, I look for the following three things:

1. Work ethic
2. Intellect
3. Cultural fit

To build a thriving law practice, it's a given that everyone has to be smart and hard working. Over the years, I've learned, unfortunately, that people can be smart, hardworking, deceitful, and disloyal. Of the lawyers who suddenly left my practice, taking their clients with them as well as attempting to take some of mine, one of those lawyers was deceitful. When policy issues came up, he told me that he had my back and was looking out for the Firm. I should have known better.

I still believe that most people are trustworthy. I'm not willing to let a bad apple poison my view of humanity. Still, I've learned that cultural fit is essential to a healthy practice and that I must adhere to a zero-tolerance policy regarding dishonesty. There is a saying "hire slow, fire fast." When your instincts are telling you someone is not honest or even a good fit, you are almost always right. Pull the trigger, and you will be happier once you do. The rest of the team around you will be happier too. You might be surprised that the others saw a bad fit before you did, and although they won't say it, they are happily wondering what took you so long.

For me, fit means embracing integrity, saying what you are going to do and doing it, keeping your commitments, serving clients, good lawyering, and having fun. I hire to fit that profile as well as to round out my suite of services and get the work done. When a person with this profile crosses my path, I am always hiring.

Attract—Hire—Retain

Smart employees with a good work ethic and cultural fit aren't necessarily easy to find. You must sell your practice to potential employees as much as you have to sell it to potential clients. Your reputation, consisting of what your employees and your clients say about you, is your best-selling tool—or not. If you are a lousy boss or don't provide a good place to work, it's hard to hide that, especially with social media. I guard the reputation of our Firm as if it's a family member.

To find potential candidates, I utilize headhunters, ads on our website, networking, and various career development centers. Early on in my business, candidates were difficult to find and the applicant pool was light. Lately, perhaps the last five years or so, we have had overwhelming interest. That has more to do with the maturity of the Firm than anything else, such as the economy. Early on, we were a bigger risk. Now that we are an established, successful firm, it is easier to sell.

An interview at The Lynch Law Group involves both talking and listening. It includes a discussion of the Firm's mission, vision, and values, and a discussion of the four areas of fulfillment we strive to achieve. I share my bedrock principles, especially the one about keeping promises to clients. And I commit to keeping my promises to my employees as well. Anything less is hypocritical. I talk about our culture and how hard we work to make The Lynch Law Group a great place to work. I talk about our commitment to development and helping lawyers build a book of business. I talk about the importance of family, work-life balance, and the philosophy that a happy lawyer is a better lawyer.

Once I make a good hire, I know it is my responsibility to retain that employee. High turnover is expensive, disruptive, and a threat to your reputation. However, know that it is okay when employees leave. It is not always a good *mutual* fit. You won't always know that in an interview, but it is almost always best for the organization. When someone leaves by his or her own decision, or if you have to show them the door, you will almost always find that the rest of your team will say "thank God" or "what took you so long?"

The Lynch Law Group engages in several initiatives to build a team that not only works hard but also enjoys each other as people. For example, we have gone to a Pittsburgh Pirates baseball game. We've gone to a shooting club, hired instructors, and learned to shoot handguns and shotguns. And, we have an annual summer family picnic with games, races, contests, and lots of eating and drinking. These events go a long way in creating a fun environment, a short distraction from the work, and a family atmosphere.

Everyone, including me, meets with direct reports at least twice per year. This is a time for two-way feedback. We encourage everyone to give feedback on the Firm and share suggestions for improvement. Once a year, I ask all employees to provide a list of at least three things that if they had all the time and money in the world, they would implement to make the Firm a better place to work. Every two weeks, we have a 90-minute practice development meeting with our lawyers. This is my time to teach and mentor. As a group, we explore the principles behind effective business development, share stories, and hold each other accountable to our goals and objectives. We encourage and challenge one another. We focus on the behaviors that can help us to grow—those involved in selling and those involved in becoming better lawyers.

The Lynch Law Group's monthly internal newsletter encourages a family feel and sense of belonging at the Firm. I write a brief reflective article, but the highest value comes from people contributing photos, stories, and information such as "what you don't know about me." The newsletter is also a great place for what I call notables. Whether you call them notables, shout-outs, kudos, accolades, or something else, people need to hear them, and the people who performed the good deed like to be mentioned.

MOTIVATION AND MONEY

As you know, lawyers need to be motivated to both generate work (develop business for the firm) and produce the work (provide excellent legal services). There is always a tension between these two activities. I put it this way: When you are out there getting the work, you are not in the office doing the work. And when you are in the office doing the work, you are not out there getting the work.

As mentioned in Chapter 2, at our Firm, we help to motivate each other by setting goals for networking events, first-time appointments (FTAs), referral sources, and potential new clients. We keep track of these key-performance indicators (KPIs). We identify and measure behaviors that we know lead to success, creating an achievement-oriented culture. We provide coaching and feedback to each other. We have accountability partners and hold each other accountable to our self-imposed goals.

We also provide financial incentives for lawyers to meet goals in both business development and billable hours. Each lawyer receives a salary, tied to a base level of expectation. Lawyers can earn bonuses, based on one of two factors. They can earn a bonus on the percentage of business they bring in. (I offer this incentive immediately after hiring and with the very first dollar, rather than after a certain number of billable hours or amount of business, as some firms do.) Lawyers can also earn a bonus on the number of billable hours worked above and beyond the budgeted number agreed upon in advance.

LEADERSHIP LESSONS LEARNED

Activities of building and maintaining an effective and satisfied team take time away from business development and client service, but they are equally important.

In any law firm, the different practice areas tend to operate as mini law firms or silos. Each silo has a lead lawyer, paralegal, administrative personnel, and associate lawyers. While that silo will share the assistance of human resources, accounting, billing, and marketing, it will still operate much like a silo. For a team to function effectively, the lead lawyer in any silo needs to engage his or her people on multiple levels. That lead lawyer must invest the time to get to know direct reports, engage socially, and talk about things other than work. The managing partner must do the same for the lead lawyers who report to him or her. The managing partner must know the members of the firm as people as well as professionals.

In a business in which generating new business is a constant demand, the need to build relationships with team members can feel like a distraction. Make no mistake, the effort you put into engaging your team is not a distraction; it's an investment. I learned this the hard way.

The sudden and unethical departure of those aforementioned five lawyers and three administrative professionals propelled me to reflect and assess many things about my practice, including my leadership behavior. I realize now that I had become apathetic in my leadership and had stopped investing in my team. Another leader—one with nefarious motives—stepped in. I lost a team I had built, taught, and mentored, as well as the business they took with them.

That painful betrayal taught me to be a better leader, husband, and father. Among the top things I learned was that good leadership communicates *acceptance* in a way I had not understood.

I've come to appreciate that not everyone will do things my way, and not everyone has the same definition of excellence. A leader has to define excellence. The team has to execute the tasks to get there. I've learned that not everyone is an A player, and not all A players are the same. Having a different commitment to excellence does not make a person a B player—just a different player. Not everyone is as passionate as me about the practice of law, the building of a book of business, and the creation of a culture that is rewarding on multiple levels. I have also learned that all businesses need B players. Businesses can't exist without them, and they need to be embraced, respected, mentored, and appreciated.

I had held former team members to a standard of commitment that I defined, not one that they embraced. When those team members didn't meet my standard, I became resentful, distant, and apathetic. Working at our Firm stopped being fun, and a leadership gap opened. While paying a high price for that gap, the exodus also served as a cleansing, and may well be the best thing that could have happened to me both professionally and personally.

What was missing with the group that departed was a cultural fit based on the defining principles described in Chapter 2. Now I hire to a new standard; I hire based on those principles and consider them a framework in which people can express their individuality. When I delegate, I define the result I want but not the path to get there. I trust my team members to accomplish the job their way, within the framework of the Principles.

And I accept that people are not perfect, and the work will never be done exactly as I would do it myself, but that's okay. I don't need to control that. I need to let the work get out the door. You must decide whether to do everything yourself— and many do it this way—and not be able to grow, or delegate tasks to others, which will allow you to grow. If you decide to delegate, you may find that quality might actually improve because of more focused knowledge and/or pride in personal accountability. Of course, quality does not always improve, and you are going to have to be okay with that as long as the baseline standards are met. I have learned to have more patience, and consequently I have found that when I hire well, invest in my team members, and then trust them to do high quality work, everybody wins—the client, the team members, and the Firm.

MENTOR AND MITIGATE RISK

Good leaders are, by definition, good mentors. Managing partners mentor growing team members, teaching them how to be good lawyers and how to be successful businesspeople. In other words, they share the secrets they've learned through their own struggles. Because of a nasty experience, I'm sensitive to the fact that I might do everything right as a leader, and in doing so, enable the people in whom I've invested, to leave. They might take off to start their own firms, and that is okay. People leave.

It would be easy to live with a sense of paranoia and mistrust, but I choose not to do that. Life is short, and I don't want to live without trusting others. I have always had an abundance mentality, believing there is plenty of work for everyone and that what we give comes back to us multiplied. I did not let the "departure" change that. This doesn't mean I haven't learned some lessons about protecting my book of business.

When I worked at Reed Smith, I noticed that some of the senior partners jealously guarded their clients from impatient and untrustworthy younger lawyers. They delegated *work* but not the *relationship* with the client. I made the mistake of trusting lawyers to manage relationships. In the "departure," some of the lawyers stole a few of my clients.

Today, I'm careful to assure the clients I've attracted to think of me as their lawyer, even if one of my colleagues does much of the actual work. I maintain the relationships. This can be a daunting task, especially as your book of business grows. If you have a $1 million book of business, managing every relationship is impossible. The trick is to pick and choose the clients that will continue to give you years of regular business. There is a saying in business that 20% of customers contribute to 80% of profit. Those are the relationships you want to constantly and continuously cultivate. And the relationships you allow to be nurtured by others will not be your relationships for long. That is okay. You cannot, and don't want to, maintain every possible relationship. I assure you, the abundance mentality works. For every client I have lost due to relinquishing the management of the relationship, I have gained ten more.

Obviously, if I'm doing a good job of growing my business, I have to delegate to others—and I can't be suspicious of every interaction my lawyers have with clients. I can and do talk to employees about the ethics involved in lawyer/client relationships. As early as the first interview, I tell associates that I plan to invest in them and share the secrets of what I did to get where I am. I tell them that I hope they will stay with The Lynch Law Group forever, but I'll understand if they decide to go on their own at some point. I make it clear that, in that case, I expect them to honor business development success and to leave my clients with me. I also tell them that I want them to learn along the way and be the best lawyer they can be. If they ever decide to leave, they are still a reflection of me and the time they have spent with me.

I have been blessed, and I believe that investing in others is a way to give back, to contribute to their success. Nearly all people will honor your investment in them as long as you communicate clear expectations. I strive to teach integrity with my words and the example I set in every relationship. If you, however, are inclined to build your practice with low standards of ethics and integrity, think again. If you think that working with a rainmaker for a couple of years and then trying to steal business on your way out the door is a pathway to success, you are wrong. You will be known as deceitful, dishonest, and disloyal. Who wants that in their lawyer? You will attract like-minded people and you will always need to watch your back. In other words, if you steal to reach the top, you'll have good reason to be paranoid when you get there.

Rather, I believe in working hard to earn what you achieve. Putting in the time to do what it takes to be great will increase your chances of being great. From the employer's perspective, reward hard work and it will keep coming. Applaud when your employees do well and it will encourage similar standards. Teach young lawyers and you will be respected. Compliment often. Communicate clearly and manage expectations. You will get what you tolerate, so maintain your standards. And most of all, CARE. To paraphrase Theodore Roosevelt, employees do not care how much you know until they know how much you care.

CHAPTER 12

TYING IT ALL TOGETHER

B Y THE TIME I WAS IN MY MID-40S and had been running a successful law practice for 13 years, I had strong opinions about how to succeed in building and servicing an above-average book of business. I had researched, studied, and practiced behaviors that would move me in the right direction. I had thought carefully about what principles should undergird these behaviors. I disciplined myself to adhere to the behaviors and principles. My originations were in excess of $1 million, giving me confidence that I knew the path to success.

As the managing member of our Firm, it was in my best interest to mentor those on my team. Accordingly, I spent a great deal of energy figuring out how to articulate best practices for developing a book of business. Business development meetings and conversations were (and are) a regular feature in the rhythm of our Firm. Intentional lessons and conversations about best practices for life were (and are) also regular features of my and Susan's life with our children.

When the five partner-level lawyers of the Firm came into my office to announce, "We're leaving," I had to step back and reexamine everything I'd been espousing with such confidence. You might remember some of the questions I asked myself, detailed in Chapter 1:

- Is it possible to make lawyering fun *and* successful?

- Is it possible in this business to build relationships that satisfy?

- What elements make up a winning business strategy and practice?

- How do I build a professional, productive, and loyal team?

- How do I get work done for clients while chasing new business?

- Assuming it is ineffective to sell on price and quality (because everyone does), how do I distinguish myself?

- How do I build a network that feeds me business rather than just taking up my time?

- Do today's clients want transactions or experiences? How do I deliver the latter?

- What's the right balance between the personal and professional? How do I achieve this balance in the hours I have each week?

Obviously, these questions are deeper and more profound than the simple question, "What went wrong with my relationship with these five lawyers?" At the time, I was already working with a book coach in the beginning stages of this book. When the betrayal and exodus of more than 50% of my staff occurred, I had deep and profound questions.

Even as I struggled, I knew at a deep level that this event, in addition to being a crisis, was also an opportunity to clarify and test my own attitudes and actions about success. Was I all talk, or did I have genuine insights about success? Were the first 13 years just luck? Would I stop growing because of this setback or live out the lessons I was constantly teaching to my team, my children, and myself? Did I have any credibility to write a book? At the time, it certainly didn't feel like it. It felt more like everything I had built had just been stolen by a thief in the dark of the night (oh, that's right; it was).

Now, with fresh confidence, I'm putting the finishing touches on this book. I feel time-and-hardship tested and have enjoyed the journey of sharing what I know with you.

I want to emphasize my central principle, which is that, above all, lawyering is a relationship business. A good lawyer knows the law and applies the law as an art *on behalf of people*. If you want an above-average book of business, you will have to invest a great deal of time, energy, and money in face-to-face interactions with clients and referral sources. Neither shortcuts nor gimmicks can take the place of this investment. If your plan to build a book of business was to sit behind your desk and make a few clicks on social media websites while business comes your way, this was the right book for you to read. The good news is, if you discipline yourself and consistently invest in the right behaviors, the business will come.

Taken by themselves, the behaviors on which I've built my business aren't unique to me. You can find plenty of books on choosing a niche, setting goals, perfecting your pitch, establishing a network, caring for your clients, and establishing a practice. I don't claim to have a secret sauce in these areas. The secret sauce boils down, pure and simple, to discipline. You must perform the behaviors consistently over time, both on days you feel like it and days you don't. It is a way of life.

The day-in and day-out part of building a successful business can be tedious and exhausting, simply because the need to perform these behaviors never ends—it's rigorous. This is why so many people either don't or can't do it.

When I feel tempted to slack off from the rigorous work, I simply dig in. I have been that way all my life. When I read Angela Duckworth's book, *Grit*, I was pleased to find that she established in a scientific fashion my approach to hard work and success. Duckworth's research reveals that the people most likely to succeed are not necessarily those with the highest IQ or the most natural ability. The people most likely to succeed are those with the most grit, which she defines as the combination of passion and perseverance for a singularly important goal. While we can't control our IQ, we can control our grit. If I had my way, we'd talk about IQ (intelligence quotient), EQ (emotional quotient), and GQ (grit quotient) as essential attributes leading to success.

I am convinced that grit is essential for success in any long-term endeavor, but that doesn't mean life has to be all about gritting our teeth. For me, the principles that undergird my day-to-day behaviors infuse every day with opportunity, excitement, and inspiration.

I pulled away from the crowd with the principle I learned from an early mentor at Reed Smith: Every client is a friend and every friend is a client. Envisioning every friend as a client, rather than an off-limits individual, broadens my possibility of potential client interactions exponentially. It requires me to stretch for the highest standards of ethics and service.

Envisioning every client as a friend, rather than merely as a source of income, allows me to seek to know the whole person, opening doors for interesting interactions and conversations as I perform my work. These rich interactions take so much of the tedium out of the constant networking behaviors that are essential to building a book of business. It becomes fulfilling and meaningful. When every client is a friend, I grow as a person while serving my clients.

With the perspective that every friend is a client and every client is a friend, my professional life and personal life become intertwined. I am not constantly feeling that one aspect of life is interfering with the other. In fact, I feel the opposite. This perspective drives me to invest as intentionally in each member of my family as I do with a potential or long-standing client. I don't take any of the people in my life for granted.

Blending these two aspects of life requires balance and can be tricky, but I wouldn't have it any other way. Susan and our children are enriched in so many ways by the interactions and activities we have with clients. Because I seek to interact with clients according to the client's issues, our kids are exposed to a variety of experiences that would not necessarily come naturally to our family. I've shared the example of that mission trip Danny took to the Dominican Republic. You'll remember that Danny claims his mission experience changed his life.

Thinking of every friend as a client and every client as a friend naturally motivates me to strive for two goals: First, I am motivated to judge all my work against the standard of excellent friendship. Excellence means that I say what I am going to do, and I do it. I keep my word. I always respond in a timely manner and deliver the highest quality legal work. Second, I am motivated to make every day and every interaction fun. If my business and personal life are inextricably intertwined, I don't need to relegate my positive energy and fun to nonwork hours. Thus, I work hard and I play hard. I model this for my team and for my children.

I strive to make life fun because I like fun—but also because I know that people and potential clients are attracted to fun. In my view, a day is a success if I've had fun and made money; both ingredients are needed for a great day.

You will remember that Simon Sinek reminds us that consumers seek *experiences* rather than *transactions* from their providers. I believe lawyers can provide experiences by ensuring their interactions with clients are sincere, creative, and fun. My greatest assets in this pursuit are positive energy, curiosity, and the willingness to learn and try out new things. Anyone can cultivate these assets, inside the office as well as outside.

The pages of this book reveal my answers to the deep questions I asked myself in response to the event that shook my world three years ago. I will end with the answers to two of my top questions:

- It's not only possible to have a law practice that is fun and successful. In fact, fun experiences with clients and potential clients are a productive path to a bigger book of business.

- It's absolutely possible to have business relationships that satisfy. In fact, building relationships is the key way to distinguish yourself from other lawyers. This is the road to the *experiences* that consumers seek. Anything else is simply a transaction.

I hope that as you build your book of business, you'll return to these pages often. Read the step-by-step chapters and practice the behaviors. Undergird those behaviors with the principles described in Chapter 2. Set goals and work hard to achieve them. Develop your sense of curiosity and your skills in listening. Think of lawyering as a game that allows you to meet new people, try out new things, and undertake adventures. Have fun. Don't be afraid to be great. Most of all, invest in relationships. Think of those relationships as friendships and give them your very best.

Do these things and your book of business will grow.

ABOUT THE AUTHOR

AN ATTORNEY FOR OVER 25 YEARS, Dan Lynch is the Founder and Managing Partner of The Lynch Law Group. His areas of strength and experience include securities litigation; business succession planning; employment law counseling and litigation; commercial litigation; mergers and acquisitions; and general corporate transactions. Dan is a success-driven leader with superior organization and communication skills. He has practical business experience, a solid work ethic, and brings an entrepreneurial approach to his practice of law. He is a passionate student of the principles and behaviors that lead to business growth in professional services. His $1 million+ book of business is a testament to his knowledge and discipline in this area.

Before starting his own law firm, Dan was Vice President and General Counsel for Pittsburgh Logistics Systems, Inc., a middle-market company based in Rochester, Pennsylvania, engaged in third-party logistics. In this role, Dan was responsible for the legal department, managing a full range of legal services and solutions in all areas of the business. The human resources department, security, and building facilities all reported to Dan, and he reported to the CEO.

Prior to his employment at Pittsburgh Logistics Systems, Dan was the CEO of 3e Software, Inc., a start-up company located in Pittsburgh, Pennsylvania, that provided software to e-marketplaces. As the CEO, Dan was responsible for the overall management of the company, which included operations, marketing, sales, finance, product development, and information technology. Dan established the organizational structure and strategic direction of the company, raised the seed financing, managed the financial performance and forecasting, and hired and led the management team.

Early in his career, Dan was a practicing lawyer for six years at Reed Smith LLP, an international law firm with over 2,000 lawyers headquartered in Pittsburgh, Pennsylvania. Dan focused his practice on complex commercial litigation with an emphasis in the areas of technology, financial services, civil RICO, shareholder derivative actions, and the First Amendment. While at Reed Smith, Dan was responsible for managing his own caseload, generating new business, managing client relations, and staffing the majority of his cases.

He joined Reed Smith after completing a one-year clerkship for the Honorable James H. Brickley, Justice of the Michigan Supreme Court, and a one-year clerkship for the Honorable Carol Los Mansmann of the United States Court of Appeals for the Third Circuit.

Dan and his family reside in Fombell, Pennsylvania. He enjoys traveling, competing in triathlons; playing soccer and golf; hiking and other outdoor activities; reading, cooking and spending time with his wife and four children. Dan has served on numerous boards and currently serves as a board member for the Pittsburgh Venture Capital Association and as chairman of the North Catholic High School Parent Communication Committee.

To Book Dan to Speak to Your Group

To schedule Dan to speak to your group on *Building a Million Dollar Book of Business,* and the principles and behaviors that lead to a successful law practice, contact him at:

Website ......: www.LynchLaw-Group.com

Email ....: DLynch@LynchLaw-Group.com

LinkedIn......: www.linkedin.com/in/danielplynch1/

Phone ....: 724-776-8000

www.ingramcontent.com/pod-product-compliance
Lightning Source LLC
Chambersburg PA
CBHW071858200326
41519CB00016B/4441